Regimen Sanitatis, the Rule of Health; a Gaelic Medical Manuscript of the Early Sixteenth Century or Perhaps Older From the Vade Mecum of the Famous Macbeaths, Physicians to the Lords of the Isles and the Kings of Scotland for Several Centuries

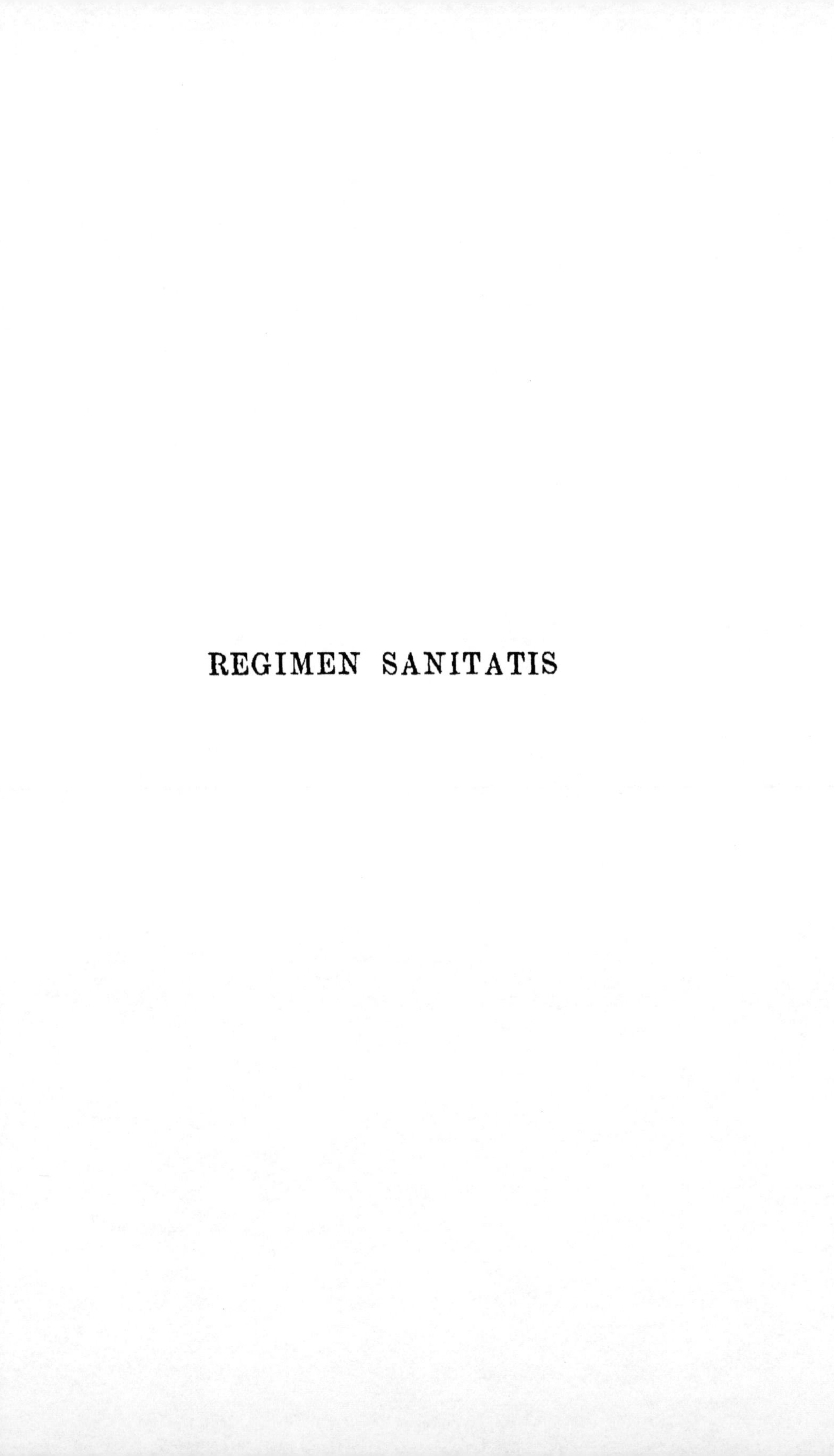

REGIMEN SANITATIS

REGIMEN SANITATIS

THE RULE OF HEALTH

A Gaelic Medical Manuscript of the Early Sixteenth Century or perhaps older

FROM

THE VADE MECUM OF THE FAMOUS MACBEATHS

PHYSICIANS TO THE LORDS OF THE ISLES AND THE KINGS OF SCOTLAND FOR SEVERAL CENTURIES

BY

H. CAMERON GILLIES, M.D.

DEDICATED TO JOHN FOURTH MARQUIS OF BUTE

PRINTED FOR THE AUTHOR BY

ROBERT MACLEHOSE & CO. LTD.

UNIVERSITY PRESS, GLASGOW

1911

DEDICATED TO

JOHN, FOURTH MARQUIS OF BUTE

An t'-Ochdamh Iarla Bhoite

PREFACE.

THIS is the first definite effort to restore our old Gaelic Medical Manuscripts which have lain unknown for so many centuries.

From the national-historical point of view the Text is very interesting, while from the medical-historical it is even more so, and from the scholar's point it must be of distinct importance. I have tried to keep my eyes open in these three directions

I have been impelled to endeavour to do this work from a strong feeling that it ought to be done—that it was indeed, for long years, calling to be done. My instinctive devotion to my native language and the exceptional combination, with that, of my Medical training and my very big experience, seemed to make the call imperative that I should undertake the work, for this necessary combination in the life of one person does not occur very often

I was also encouraged by the patriotic sympathy and enthusiasm of a nobleman who does his heredity full honour by showing his keen interest in the tradition and literature of his race, and particularly in the direction which this effort so far realises.

Very much remains to be done in this way, and it must be undertaken soon, because some of these MSS. are very far gone in decay—especially those written on paper. This work may encourage, as it certainly will assist, such as may wish to work in this field.

Hearty thanks are due to the Publishers, who did this difficult work sympathetically and admirably.

LONDON, *December* 1910

CONTENTS.

INTRODUCTION.

THIS tract *Regimen Sanitatis* or the Rule of Health is from a Gaelic Medical Manuscript which I found at the British Museum. The MS (catalogued as Add 15582) consists of sixty-two vellum folios, the same size as is here reproduced. The cover is skin-covered board ornamented by simple straight-line devices The front board has two sides of the original pair of silver clasps still attached, the other parts are wanting The vellum is in a very fair state of preservation, and the writing, as may be seen from the photographic reproduction, is quite legible Without doubt this book belonged to John MacBeath, one of the very remarkable family of that name who were hereditary physicians to the Lords of the Isles and to the Kings of Scotland for several centuries The volume remained in the MacBeath family for many generations, but how it found its way into England, I fear, cannot now be surely known. The only indication is that it was "purchased of Thos. Rodd 9th August 1845"—by the Museum—but how it came into Rodd's hands is not known There is another MacBeath book also lying here (catalogued as Add 15403), a smaller vellum treating of Materia Medica. It also was got through Rodd, a well-known London bookseller who took up his father's business in 1821, and died 1849. In this volume, on inserted paper leaves in the front, occur these statements (1) "Presented by Sir Wm. Betham [to the Duke of Sussex ?] May 24th 1827—MS on Botany in the Irish character", (2) "Purchased at the Sussex Sale 31st July 1844 by Thorpe and of him (through Rodd) for B M. 10 Aug 1845." It is very likely that the two volumes came by the same way, so far. Sir Wm. Betham was Keeper of the Records of Dublin Castle from 1805 onwards until he was made Ulster King of Arms in 1820 He was devoted to philology and to the Gaelic language especially, and wrote extensively upon Keltic subjects He died at Blackrock near Dublin in 1853 The Duke of Sussex (1773-1846) was sixth son of George III. and a president of the Royal Society

THE MACBEATHS

The only methodical attempts as yet made to endeavour to get the long history of this family into anything like order have been (1) by Professor Mackinnon in two valuable articles written to the *Edinburgh Medical Journal* in 1896, (2) by myself in an essay written for the Caledonian Medical Society in 1902, published in the Society's *Journal* for April of that year, and (3) by Professor Mackinnon again upon "The Genealogy of the MacBeths or Beatons of Islay and Mull," which was published in the same *Journal* (*C.M J*) in July of the same year I here summarise these efforts, and try to get them into such order as I may be able to—with any additional facts I may have lately culled. This will give a more direct and intelligent interest to the text than could be possible without it It will also serve as a basis for further investigation and addition.

The name MacBeath (as I here prefer it) is very variously written in the old manuscripts and in books It is Mac-bead, *Book of Deer* 11th cent, M'Betha 1408, Beatone 1511, Meg Beth 1563, Micbhethadh 1587, MacBeath 1609, Beatoun 1638, M'Bethadh 1657, Betonus 1674, Bettounus 1677, Beda 1680—but older far—Maigbheta 1701, Maig Bhetha 1708 In the MSS. of the Advocates' Library the dates of which are not yet fixed, it occurs as Betune II, Meigbetadh IV, Maigbheta V, Magbeta XX, Makbetathe, M'Veagh Beattoun and Beattounne XXI It has become Peudan (Peden) in Skye and Biotun in Mull Bethune also occurs associated with the MacBeaths, but as this family is said to have come from Fife it is doubtful if they were at all related in name or blood. There may have been an overlapping or an intermixture of the names, but the basic name is that given.

The true forms of the family name, such as Bead, Beda, Macbheatha and Macbheathadh, mean "Son of life," following a very old form of Gaelic naming, perhaps the oldest, many others of which remain with us to the present day.

Other important facts relating to this family are, in—

1379 Farquhar (medicus regis) had a grant from Prince Alexander Stuart ("The Wolf of Badenoch") of the lands of Melness and Hope, and in—

1386. Ferchard Leiche, "Farquhar the physician," got in heritage from King Robert II. the islands of Jura, Calwa, Sanda, Ellangawne, Ellanwillighe, Ellanrone, Ellanehoga, Ellanequochra, Ellanegelye, Ellaneyefe, and all the islands between Rowestorenastyngho and Rowearmadale—Rudh' a' Stóir an Assaint and Rudh' Armadail

1408. Fercos Macbetha witnesses, and almost certainly draws, a deed of land-grant in Islay to "Brian Vicaire Mhag-aodh" from "McDomhnaill"—the Macdonald of the Isles who led the Highlanders at the battle of Harlaw, 24th July, 1411 His father, John, Lord of the Isles, was married to Lady Margaret Stuart, daughter of Robert II This deed is reproduced in *Nat MSS Scot.* Vol. ii No. lix, and in *The Book of Islay*, and in the *C M J.* for April, 1902 The lands here granted are situated in the Oa extending across from Kilneachtoin to Laggan Bay.

1511. Donold M'Donachy or M'Corrachie (simply the same name mis-written because most likely mis-spoken), "descendit frae Farquhar Leiche," resigned the lands of Melness and Hope and all the lands of Strathnaver, in favour of the Chief of the Mackays Donnachadh (Duncan) was a favourite name with the MacBeaths, and the M'Donachy, M'Corrachie (for MacDhonnachaidh) and the Connachers of Lorn are one and the same name Donchad M'Meic Bead occurs in *The Book of Deer*

Duncan Conacher wrote a medical work at Dunollie in this same year, which is still extant.

In 1511 a David Beatone was among the "Nomina incorporatorum" of the University of Glasgow, and from that time onwards through three centuries the Roll contains such names as Johannus Beatonus, Fergus Betonius, Duncan Beatonus, Donaldus Beatonus, etc.

1563 Another Tract of this same MS, mostly surgical, was written for John MacBeath by David O'Kearny It was published, *C M J* April, 1902.

1587. Under this date there is a Gaelic entry in the Laing MS (Adv xxi.) that the book then belonged to Gilcolum son of Gilanders son of Donald MacBeath.

In Adv iii. (which I have at the B M, by the courtesy of the Directors, for the purpose of reference) there occurs on the second folio from the end, in the top margin, **Misi Gilla Col[aim]** *I am Gilla-colum.*

1598. The MS was in possession of James MacBeath at Tain It was evidently lent him by John, the real owner, whose mother had in that year made a journey to Islay—*C.M J*

1609 James VI confirms to Fergus M'Beath by charter certain lands in the Oa of Islay which his family had held from the Lords of the Isles in virtue of their office as hereditary physicians "ab omni hominum memoria" The full text of the charter is given in the *C.M J*

1629 These lands were sold by John the son of Fergus to the Lord Lorne of the time and the charter found its way to Inveraray, where it is preserved.

1638 A James Betoun, "doctor of physicke," made a "voyage" from Edinburgh to Islay professionally twice, as would seem, in this year. In the Accounts of Colin and George Campbell—brothers and curators successively of John Campbell Fiar of Calder (1638-1653)—there appears an item of payment to the said James of £266 13s 4d. for his first journey "as his ticket of rescate bearis," and of £178 8s. for the second, and a further sum of £101 6s 8d. paid to Patrick Hepburn "for drogis that went in Doctour Beatoune his companie to Illa"

1657. The Laing MS then belonged to a Donald MacBeath as an entry shows.

1657. John, a distinguished member of the Mull branch—the famous *Ollamh Muileach*, died He was buried in Iona, where Donald Beaton in 1674 placed a slab to his memory bearing the inscription "Joannes Betonus, Maclenorum familie medicus qui mortuus est 19 Novembris 1657."

1671. Ιοαννυς Βεττοννυς possessed the MS Adv. iii., for he says εγραπε το χειρ αυτων, 1671, evidently intended to mean "written with his own hand," and E M'B appears in a small circular mended patch on the inside of the cover

1700 Martin wrote his *Travels*, where he makes interesting references to the Beatons He states among other things that "Dr Beaton the famous physician of Mull" was sitting on the upper deck of the *Florida*, one of the vessels of the Spanish Armada, when it was blown up in the bay of Tobermory in 1588, but that he escaped unhurt.

1701. A John MacBeath possessed the MS Adv v.

1708. This MS. (15582) was in the possession of John MacBeath. His name is written under 25th May of that year.

1710 The same name is written under "20 die Junii." Although the writing of this name and that of 1708 are very different, it is almost certainly that of the same John

1778. The Rev. Thomas White of Liberton who married a Miss Bethune of Skye wrote a pamphlet giving a genealogy of the Skye branch from a manuscript to which he had access This was reprinted by Mackenzie of Glasgow in 1887 for a Mr. Kenneth Maclennan.

1784. The Rev. Donald Macqueen gave a Gaelic copy of the *Lilium Medicinae*, which belonged to the Beatons "for five generations before," to the Society of Antiquaries.

THE SUBSTANCE OF THE TEXT

Even if this book may not add very much to the sum of our present medical knowledge it is nevertheless of extreme interest from the human and historical aspect as well as from the point of view of the physician and the scholar To find men in the far North and in the Western Isles of Scotland who, in those early centuries, were familiar with, and had well digested all that was best in the medical literature of Greece and Rome and Araby is more than, let us say, Lord Macaulay would give them credit for, and it would surely surprise Samuel Johnson to find that there was a great mass of Gaelic scientific writing lying unknown, for long ages, before he declared that there was not one page in the language beyond a hundred years old. It was so, however, even if Dr. Johnson did not know, and even if Lord Macaulay to his utter discredit did not want to

The generalisations of the first chapter are so completely comprehensive and yet so extremely precise and logical, that we may doubt if they have ever been, or can be, improved upon. *Conservatiuum*, *Preservatiuum*, and *Reductiuum* round the whole duty of man regarding his health in the most perfect way, and perhaps in the very best form of words *Conservatiuum* is the duty of those in health, or, as we might say, an intelligent understanding of the conditions of health and life, and a rightly careful application of this most useful and saving knowledge, to conserve the healthful state, is the first and highest duty of everyone. That is what Conservation means, or as Dr. Standish O'Grady has put it with almost a stroke of genius, "Keep as you are"

Preservatiuum, again, is for those who know by any signs that they are departing from the fully healthy state and are going into unhealth and weakness "that is proper and necessary" for them, and very urgently so, if they are to save themselves from a much worse state

Reductiuum is for those who, failing to apply their common sense in the earlier, easier positions, must now be *led back*, through suffering and sorrow and loss and expense, the same way as that by which they ignorantly or foolishly came down—back to and through the *Preservatiuum* or "fore-seeing" position where they could have saved themselves before, and up to the position at which *Conservatiuum* would have made their decline and dis-ease impossible—that is, if they ever get back there again How very often do we hear a man say, "Since that last illness, I have not been myself at all, I find I must be careful now." This is the very essence of wisdom, but it has been dearly bought—perfection through suffering surely, for very much less "care" at the proper time would have saved him from the whole catastrophe Much more rarely we hear, "Since that last illness I have been a new man" This simply means that a man who has been drawing too much upon his life and health has been "pulled up," and through long and careful *Reductio* he has been led back fortunately to his first position of apparently good health *Conservatiuum* is the position for thoughtful, sensible men. *Preservatiuum* is the position at which natural warnings show themselves and should be understood and obeyed. *Reductiuum* is the whip-lash of compulsion which comes really to save and not to destroy, but which even in the best event can only attain, through suffering and sore uphill travail, to the position of less or more of the health which with some sense should never have been lost or departed from.

The sensefulness of this single chapter alone, if people would only understand and act upon it, would fully justify the labour and expense entailed by this work, apart altogether from its aim in other directions

I do not analyse the contents of the Tract. It will reveal itself It is full of wisdom—the filtrate, so to say, of a thousand years of very clear thought, and the essence of writings that are permanent. The very admirable morning "toilet" of the Third Chapter is, however, commended to the attention of such as perhaps may be disposed to believe Lord Macaulay's gross travesty of the personal habits of his own people. We must remember that this was before the advent of the household bath and the tooth-brush. It is therefore a very excellent and very wholesome direction, indeed.

THE GENESIS OF THE BOOK

John MacBeath (and I here use his name as representative of the whole family, others of them doubtless contributing also) kept a Note Book, a *Vade Mecum*, in which he stored the sum and essence of his reading, compiled and translated from the many ancient authors which we know he had in his possession He added pertinent comments and observations of his own, based upon his necessarily wide experience. All this was set down in the Scottish Gaelic of the time, which really did not differ very much from the Irish language of the same period. The compilation was not intended for publication, but was simply a practical *memoriola* such as many thoughtful physicians keep even in our day and place, when it is not nearly so necessary as it was in the MacBeaths' time and circumstances He gave his manuscripts over to a professional Irish scribe in order that the substance might be written in the best and most compact form, and that is how we have them now. This Tract was written by Aodh O'Cendainn, as is shown in the last line of column xiv. of the text. A Cairpre O'Cendamhainn wrote at least part of the Laing MS (Adv xxi) These may have been brothers A similar thing happens in the case of another Tract in this same book which was written by two O'Kearneys—David and Cairpre (*C.M.J.* April, 1902) That these men were mere copyists knowing little or nothing of Medicine or its terminology is abundantly evident from the numerous miswritings that occur throughout all their work It is also clear that they had their materials before them in Scottish Gaelic form, because we frequently find that when they take their eye off the "copy" they at once drift into the writing of Irish forms—especially of the smaller commoner words.

The MacBeath knowledge by reading seems to have included all the best that was available in their time Martin "Gent," himself a man of Skye, the interesting, observant, and very intelligent traveller, writing in 1700, states that "Fergus Beaton in South Uist possessed the following MSS, namely Avicenna, Averroes, Joannes de Vigo, Bernardus Gordonus, and several volumes of Hippocrates." These names and many others of the medical classics meet us constantly in the MacBeath writings. John might have sat for his portrait to Chaucer of his "Doctour of Phisik" in the fourteenth century, for

> Wel knewe he the olde Esculapius
> And Dioscorides and eke Rufus,
> Olde Ippocras, Haly and Gaylen,
> Serapion, Razis and Avycen,
> Averrois, Damascien and Constantyn,
> Bernard and Gatesden and Gilbertyn

It will be helpful to understand the remoter origins *Peritissimus omnium rerum Ippocras* says the postscript, column xxviii, and we may trace from this point and by this way the history of medical knowledge more directly and more appreciably than by any other path To Hippocrates, Aristotle, and Galen, and the whole immense power of the Greek intellect, medicine was always a close branch of philosophy It is not so with us now, but not long hence it must surely be so again

The disturbing but awakening power of the Macedonian conqueror led to the founding of Alexandria and its great University. This was a University in the truest sense, for it was international and catholic without restraint It had no test but knowledge and ability Gentile, Jew, and Christian were alike equal From this great centre through commercial and intellectual contact the Greek philosophy spread into Arabia and Persia and as far as India, and it had a further disseminating impulse from the banishment of the "heathen" philosophers by the first Justinian in the year 529 The effect was that a blaze of intellectual culture broke out and possessed the East for five hundred years. The great Greek writers were studied, translated and commented to an altogether wonderful extent It was in this way that came Janus "Damascenus," the Commentator of our text, and "Isaac" Judaeus and Rhases and Avicenna, Hali Averrhoes, Rufus and many others.

In the early part of the present millennium there came a great return wave which struck along the northern coasts of the Mediterranean, where many schools of learning were founded upon the Arabian models, and were greatly influenced by Arabian teachers Of these Monte-Casino, Salerno, and Montpellier were the most famous

The monastery of Monte-Casino, nearly half-way between Naples and Rome, was founded by St Benedict himself A.D 529 as is said upon the old site of a temple of Apollo Centuries later with the return of learning an infirmary was added and a school of medicine

Monks from foreign lands came there for instruction, and eminent invalids from foreign parts for treatment The most famous teacher of the School was Constantinus Africanus of Carthage (1018-1087) He introduced Arabic science and learning into Italy and Europe, and because of his universal travel and influence he was called "Orientis et Occidentis Doctor" He taught for some time at Salerno, and then became monk at Monte-Casino, where he continued his work of translating from Arabic into Latin Among his works of this kind was Hali's compendium, which he rendered under the title of *Pantegni*. It is frequently referred to in our text

Salerno (old Salernum) on the bay of the same name, some thirty miles south of Naples, was founded as a school of Philosophy and Medicine A D 1150, and was for five hundred years at the top of medical schools in Europe It was for this reason that it was nick-named "Civitas Hippocratica" It was a *practical* University, studying the symptoms of disease, diet, materia medica, and treatment in its fullest expression—not giving much attention to physiology or anatomy. The school had a very excellent effect in that its teaching mitigated and *naturalised* the rather severe doctrines of the older Greek methods of treatment, and this, without doubt, came by Arabic influence. Two great and permanent works issued from this school, namely, the *Compendium Salernitatum* and the rhymed *Regimen Sanitatis Salerni*. The former was a composite treatise, the text-book of the school, of which Joannes Platearius was part author. His part of the *Compendium* is the basis of the other MacBeath MS (Add 15403) in the British Museum. The other work is a poem, or rather a versification, the object of which was that the wisdom it conveyed could be more easily committed to, and retained in the memory. It was addressed to Robert, son of William the Conqueror, "Anglorum Regi," who was cured of a wound at Salerno in the year 1101. This was the *vade mecum* of every well-educated physician in Europe for several centuries. Sylvius, in his edition of the *Schola Salernitana* (Rotterdam, 1649), says *Nullus medicorum est qui carmina Scholae Salernitanae ore non circumferet et omni occasione non crepet*. This work is attributed to John of Milan, who was President of Salerno in his day, but the Address is from "Schola tota Salerni." That the book was in the possession of the MacBeaths there can be no doubt at all, so that if we owe the form of our text to John of Gaddesden we are indebted to the ancient School of Salernum for its substance and its whole essential character—not forgetting how much the MacBeaths themselves have added to it. The following quotation from the *Regimen*, if compared with the burden of the text, will readily show the pertinence of the statement which I have just made

Anglorum regi scribit schola tota Salerni
Si vis incolumem, si vis te vivere sanum
Curas tolle graves, irasci crede profanum
Parce mero, caenato parum, non sit tibi vanum
Surgere post epulas. Somnum fuge meridianum

Ne minctum retine Ne comprime fortiter anum.
Haec bene si serves tu longo tempore vives.
Si tibi deficiant medici, medici tibi fiant
Haec tria, mens laeta, requies, moderata dieta.

Sex horis dormire sat est juvenique senique
Septem vix pigro, nulli concedimus octo

Ex magna coena stomacho fit maxima poena
Ut sis nocte levis sit tibi coena brevis
Post coenam stabis aut passus mille meabis

Montpellier, the chief town of the province of Herault in Southern France on the Gulf of Lyons, was, like Salerno, a school of general learning, with Medicine as perhaps its highest feature The University was established by papal bull in 1289, the sex-centenary was celebrated in 1890 Gilbert the Englishman was taught here, as was also John of Gaddesden, the author of the *Rosa Anglica*, upon part of which our Text is based Bernard Gordon also, a Scot born in France, was a teacher here in the early years of the fourteenth century. He wrote the *Lilium Medicinae* which the MacBeaths possessed and rendered into Gaelic A copy of this work was presented to the library of the Society of Scottish Antiquaries in 1784, where it now lies It came from Farchai Beaton of Husabost "five generations ago"—according to the Rev. Donald Macqueen of Kilmuir who presented the book.

Montpellier was strongly under the Arabic influence, which explains how we find so very many Arabic terms in such of our Manuscripts as came by this way—especially in the names of medicinal plants and in Materia Medica generally

This very short statement of the old Schools taken with the Personal Notes will enable the reader to understand the history of the Text fairly well

THE TRANSLITERATION.

The *extension* of the Text which is arranged to face the photographs is as correct and exact as it possibly can be made. I have copied the errors of the scribe with even more care than the correct writing I am exceedingly indebted to my affectionate friend Standish H O'Grady, LL D—a **Grádhach** truly in act as in name He compared my rendering of the MS with the original, "letter for letter" as he expressed it—yes, and dot for dot This exact rendering will make the text much more valuable from the scholar's point of view, and to the student it will be always of interest to observe the many difficulties and the very frequent pitfalls which the pioneer in this kind of work had to overcome and to avoid

I have not brought the various Contractions together in one place as might have been done I thought it would be sufficient to refer to them, as they occurred, in the Notes In my Essay, which is deposited at the Library of the Society of Scottish Antiquaries, there are some ten pages of the contractions given, and a special page is given to the more important in the *Caledonian Medical Journal* for April, 1902. The novice, however, in this study will do well to make a list of them for himself, it will be easy to do so with the extension facing the original MS. writing

THE TRANSLATION.

The English rendering of the Text is very stilted—for several reasons. The diction of the old Medical Empirics which occupies the great part of the earlier chapters, and colours all the others, however simple the words may appear, is yet in concept wholly unintelligible to the mind of the present day All that could be done then was to give a rigidly literal but naked translation Then again there is the immeasureable and irreconcileable difference between the Gaelic and the English idioms. An English rendering can therefore only be a very crude compromise I have endeavoured to conserve as much of the flavour of the original as I possibly could, and yet bring as much of the sense within the English language as makes it fairly easy to follow—with a little thought and attention

THE TIME AND AGE OF THE TEXT.

This can be arrived at, but at best only approximately, by the following ways, namely.

1. By the earliest expressed date given in, or as part of, the Text We find in this same MS., and in what would seem to be *a later tract* than that of our Text, **Ocus do bi aois an tigerna antan do sgriobhadh an leabar so .i. mile bliadan ocus cuig céd ocus tri bliadna ocus tri fithid** *and the age of the Lord the time this book was written was one thousand years and five hundred and three years and three score*—1563

It is not drawing too much upon possibility nor even upon probability if we give our Text a century of existence as the handbook of the MacBeath family before it was given by this "John" to the Irish scribe O'Cendainn to copy, or the other and later tract to the O'Kearneys.

2. The form and style of the handwriting is another aid, but still only approximately The writing of *Leabhar na h'Uidhre* in its contractions and other graphical peculiarities does not differ very strongly from our Text, and its date is taken as fixed—about 1470 The same may be said of *The Book of Lismore*, and it is accepted as being of the latter part of the fifteenth century. This also is in confirmation of my deduction so far.

3. Then there is the developmental stage of the language to be considered, and this again in the matter of "Eclipsis" and other grammatical peculiarities, points to the same period

4. Finally, there is the fact that the *Rosa Anglica*, upon which our Text is based, was published in the early years of

the fourteenth century, and knowing that the MacBeaths took a high place in Medicine long before, and kept it for long after, we cannot imagine that it took more than two hundred years to come to their knowledge. Dr. O'Grady thinks the writing is of the early sixteenth century, but the late Whitley Stokes, by far the greatest Gaelic scholar of our time and perhaps of all time, placed the companion MS (15403) as of the early fifteenth or even the fourteenth century The side-light of Chaucer, already quoted from his "Doctour of Phisik" is also important in this connection, for we can hardly believe that the first physicians of Scotland were far, if at all, behind those of Chaucer's time in England in their knowledge of the authors here so freely referred to.

So, taking all these things into consideration, it does not seem too much to say that our Text is "of the Early 16th Century." I feel that it would be even safer to say the 15th century instead.

The form of the language in the Text is also of interest. If compared with the form of modern Scottish Gaelic, several points come out clearly. First, the root essentials have been, are, and remain the same—always—though other things vary and differ very much. The Eclipsis of the Strong initial Consonants **c, p, t** and even of the Medials **g, b, d** which has been so definitely developed in the later Irish language did not belong to the old language at all It is an effort to follow and to express a physiological actuality but for which expression there is really no linguistic need. We had the process fully developed in our older Scottish Gaelic, but it has most sensibly been done away with altogether, and we have no eclipsis now In my copy of the *Confession of Faith*, printed at Glasgow in 1725, such forms as **a mbpeacadh** *the sin*, **na ngcriostaidh** *of the Christians*, **na ndtrocair** *of the mercies* are met with, where the whole vocal gamut is logically, even if unnecessarily, expressed. The Irish people never went this whole logical length. It was too much to introduce a word by **mbp, ngc, ndt**—but they have stuck closely to the two letter forms of initial **mb** and **bp**, **ng** and **gc**, **nd** and **dt** Eclipsis occurs in our Text, but not regularly and not frequently, so we might fairly infer that the time of our Text was about the time of the introduction of this peculiarity in writing

The terminal inflections are fairly well preserved, but without precision or regularity—as may be seen They are carelessly and perhaps ignorantly shown and done, still they are not without interest As in the matter of eclipsis, there is in these also an apparent seeking after phonetic expression, regardless of the historical continuity of form

Aspiration of the consonants again is here only partly developed This is now complete both in Irish and in Scottish Gaelic The process has certainly deformed written Scottish Gaelic especially, which writes **h** after the consonant where Irish only uses the very much neater over-dot

All these expediences follow the "otiose" or *lazy* development which is manifest in all languages In fact, as the late Dr Macbain put it to me, it is not unlikely that mankind in days to come may be able to get along with only a few grunts The tendency is strongly in that direction. The speech of man is losing its bone and its strength, in the same way and perhaps for the same reasons as the race is losing its hair and its teeth—because it does not fully use them

PS—On 13th July, 1641, William Earl Marischal borrowed from James Beatoune of Nether Tarbett, Doctor of Medicine, and Janet Goldman, his spouse, the sum of 4000 merks upon the security of some lands in the parish of Fetteresso, for repayment of which and arrears of interest the said Mr James Beatoune raised against the Earl a successful process of apprising on the said lands before the Commissioners for the Administration of Justice on 3rd January, 1654 (*CMJ*, Jan, 1911)

It is surely interesting that when I consulted the Museum authorities as to the best man to photograph this text, they at once said "Mr Macbeth," and his name is John"

REGIMEN SANITATIS EST TRIPLEX

[illegible]

naincs dob.ul dorien comri[illegible] orig
clia anpollanigius premabuirit pr one
cio is lenicib fiuiu ractoib ocriuia
₇ acht in mano ol aoennin ... ol
... leniteb tlaig ... ol
nacsu cro dominec ₇ macurip fiuiu
le neitib fiuiu isli ₇ nacs cina le
nitib cina isle ₇ ca ₇ is poll gonol
cs. l. ouib opollainnius leniteib
fiuiu cina isli ... tlaig fel
... gohairo. aon anaic ... con
mplexa. l. o. mar ad communicat an
oamarenz ra. x. paitsil ra. ₇ con
rinic ... gorsul anpin tlaig
cina golg ... fel ... anu
... l. o. ... mar ... adim anraca
r ro ... magnum ... ad compt. l.
conol apollainnius lenitib fiuiu
... isle ₇ ... tlaig ...
golg ... adim compl. l. ... agtun
cim oocuitim aicroig cium fiuiu ...
cum ... ol apollainnius leniteib
tlig cina ... atoriug cium
a ... ol naneit ...
acomed nar lanit. r. cail ₇ canoigis
... ₇ ... ₇ ...
... ₇ ... ₇ ...
... ₇ cori
al acemn ₇ ... am ...
₇ ganab ₇ acem or mar aoubirt
... gombi ... real cor mail ...
incompt fiuiu ... gfeo
... don ... real ₇ is cori ...
uar ... fiuiu ₇ ...
m ... ₇ ...
... ol ... cor ...
incs nocona naneit, fiuiu aet nan
eit, fiuiu isle ₇ ... tlaig ...

ambel inlisa. in x. cailbrail docanaig
lec inbiid ... ...
Canoin gen tet inbiid. i. dol aeatim in
cain do clung e oirad ... cocul me
pircula ad alexandrinum Dum adhuc
apertus ocular manum ... ra
... dolam eugat ₇ iuc oclug ...
... agit ₇ ... ra cailbrail
laburius apollainnius nant ... ₇
ibt ITA comede quod sunt reliquie
... ra. i. ... cat ...
... toclug, dob ₇ agit ...
... canoig lec
... bigan do ... ro
... anem ... caitan
... anerid ... ohrair ...
... le ... bit ... angaili ... ₇
... dom ra. c. ... mar ...
e ... ra. x. ... mar ... com
... oamar ... ra. c. paitsil ra. ...
cominc ... ₇ ... nac ... re
... nac ... ₇ ...
ad ... ra. z. lebur nac ... nadad
... ca ... anbiid cor ... an
... ol ... dom ... ₇ ...
don ... anno ...
... ra. z. paitsil ...
is communica go ... nac ...
nac ... anbiid ... an ...
... ano ... an
ano ... ac ... go ... an
galt ... ₇ ... bir ...
nail ... ₇ dos ...
... an
puls domeoig ... anmr
anoi ... Coimricaig ... an cl
... ₇ ...
gan ... ₇ ... compra

dorugnad 7 gan cuirr uimpi na gabait in uirid
nacur umidh na ninnir fuine do moctugad 7 gan
urlugad na aprigtus cuminus. ni aitit in
toct doib 7 ar ni ailer go ni a tlg a ait gor
tugad fetuaidh do denam dei. bid nuirodd
enad froime ar. uman ntan ttuctur. uibr
ad 7 tuingir oile dogabail oir ergit naoi
tug innola ineanrir 7 do ant codlad 7 ta
rum. gt. aisctud lc. fer gan nim cod do
b 7 air 7 gan bl. aniod d fagb. .i. cirnd. uimpi
quin imbriuetug oir aimbuad nuiregir
mair. cuibriumuir foill rigclr. inbiad do
b 7 mgnrad nuicundigtar. girog dl. an
gnatug docomet ano ro minarwolc fin
ar docit figt fr.idim mair m. c. na donaig
nac dlt no ri b 7 ainnedirir gombid
biad air riun fagaib mailbir aglur nam
crisi 7 ir uime rir ain. ad ding gruinib nuac
b 7 ruimeisi uairruim ir. bg e mair foillt
aerioir. fa. x. parrcgul dona cantieib
fa. 3. cantic. x. .qr. fitit mar ainabair
Assgenniar ebrietatir rimel inmenre.
.i. errorerr. 1. ar frurnnac contug na
meisg. a tounuair urnni oir ge doinneigib
ir mo tart doncler. n. anfin arnagab go
mgnrad ir donaneic ib ir mo urcoidig
do 7 doinnenad 7 dona. c. fuib e intantad
sgairiur. gohimurcrac 7 ir uime rin ad
aner gu iubrir uisgi na meala do mog
agan bit ferc ainminnda nue gidg fett
ar bgan o fin dlg bat dotabair dona
sindoinib mar ad airrin gidg ad ain
ta pacaibidil labrar ofollaminug ainu
isgi 7 anfiona. Purus aqua uinum .i. add
ere ignem igni in ignis debilibz .i. ir grne
do cur a cli t inbl a conad ainmfaind
fin dotabairt dona mac amaib. gidg
aibair gomguidad dona drainib ogait
7 dont slindoine an med ualr. mar is
ainmed m.... rim cubaid doib. Adeirim

ccnet ... med uallr dotabairt donar
bidoinne ont slinoar 7 ir rin ar sligniue
ingurai toct ainmed fedor do oil 7 b
ir nadoine faidreg biodc gidg air bid
uine ont biorar. nid. ainmedirin
dotabairt doinibid mong rin dibliat 7
bid fuilinle oir a 7 ir blg atair oirbid m
ar lo eno bir ullam cumbaig mar adeir
fa. c. parrcgul dainfeirir moirium 7 ir
uime rin ad .g. air fa partcgul. c. na acom
inc nacanonur o Potus mogenciam so
luit 7 ca. ir uime rin fraifrui gim miro
im rieuit dl aitibairt t madiag 7
docit nac froimr oir ad ainta facai
bidil labrar ofollainnug ainuisgi 7 affina
Sapientes debet ri bir rohibere ne bibu
nt uinum bibat. 1. dligi nadoine legnaid
iacloini na fein ar fin dol ar. c. longad
7 mol. aitibairt deir na coda oir ad
ainta facaibidil. c. na Uinum post q
uod libet omnium ciborum. i. malum
.i. ir olc ar fin tairis gach uile bid 7 adeir
acaibidil follainnuigt ainnec iar
ribteir Uinum post cibum. i. ex re
bz magis impedientibz digest. gone
.i. donan sib ir mo toirmisg an dil a fin
dol tairis bid uirlon cotuibairt ar cuibnad
coll fuldil a e... anfin uir
an cuid dori ainta facaibidil labrar
ofollamnug ainesta ict 7 ibt magnan
ubair ... quis 7 non nimiora comedem
Oportet ut post comestionem bibat
ir hin gob tairis an caitmie ibz nic
drocht 7 nac an uair rrinnoig q Et ad bit
an ro ra rin Non. i. bibendum do
nec cibus de stomaco descendat
.i. nid dlc dol t gotuitid nanbiad
ir angcuile Ad oppositum. .i. acai ingnatb
coit cind in aaguid fo ag ol an.... q
incind 7 cairailer. Adeirim nac imgnib

Column V.

dongheadh ocus gan cuirrneacht na gaothmaireacht na truimidecht na anmfainne domothughadh ocus gan urlugadh na *apititus caininus* na tuitim tochluighthi dobeith air na leisgi indtlechta acht gof[é]tfadh stuider do dhenamh déis bídh mar do denadh roime acht amhain intan tuitius an biadh ocus tinnsgnus dileaghadh dogabhail oir éirghitt na dhetaighi inmolta intan sin ocus donít codladh ocus toirmisgit an stuider *Et* fós gan nem-codladh do beith air ocus gan blas an bídh d'fhaghbhail a cind aimsiri ar in mbrúchtaigh oir dambiadh na neithisi mar adubhrumuir foillsighter an biadh dobheith mesardha ina caindigeacht Gidhegh dligheár an gnathughadh do coimet andso muna io-olc e mar do cithfighter. *Et* adeirim mar in cétna don digh nach dlighind si beith an méidisin gombeith an biadh ar snámh sa ghaili mar bis ag lucht na meisgi ocus is uime sin aní adeir drong gurub maith beith ar meisgi uair sa mhí is brég e mar foillsighius aueróis sa dara partegul dona cantichibh sa treas cantic dég ar fhithit mar an abair *Assensus ebrietatis simel in mense est erroneus* i. as seachrannach aontughadh na meisg aon uair is in mí oir ge do na neithibh is mó tarbhaighius don tes nadurra an fín arna gabhail go mesardha is do na neithibh is mó urcoidighius dó ocus don incind ocus dona cétfadhuibh é intan tosgaighius go himurcrach ocus is uime sin adeir annsin gurub ferr uisgi na meala don droing ag ambit feithi anmfhanda na e gidhegh féttar began d'fhín deghbalaidh dotabairt do na sen-daoinibh mar adeir annsin gidhegh adeir auicina sa caibidil labrus d'fhollamhnughadh an uisgi ocus infíona *Pueris dare uinum est addere ignem igni in lignis debilibus* .i. is tine do cur a cenn tinedh a conadh anmfand fín dotabhairt dona macamhaibh. Gidhegh tabair go mesardha dona daoinibh óga e ocus don t'sendaoine an méid is áil lis maseadh is améid moir is imchubhaidh doibh e Adeirim

Column VI

condligher anméid is áil lis do tabairt dona tshenduine on thsendacht ocus is e sin an senduine mesardha thochluighes an méidh fhédus do dileaghadh ocus bis ina duine rodheisgribhidech Gidhegh an senduine on thsenordhacht ni dligheár an méidhi sin dotabhairt dó oir bidh in drong sin dibenta ocus bidh rabhaile orra ocus is beg a teas oir bidh mar lóchrand bis ullamh cum báithi mar a deirur sa cét paitegul d' *amforismorum* ocus is uime sin adeir g[alen] an sa partegul cétna a comint na canonaso *Potus indigenciam soluit, et cetera* Is uime sin fiarfuighim in roimh in chuit dligheár atabairt no inadiaigh ocus dociter nach roimpi oir adeir auicina sa caibidil labhrus d'follamhnughadh an uisgi ocus an fína *Sapiens debet sibi prohibere ne ieiunus uinum bibat* i dlighi in duine égnaidhi a caomhna fein ar fhín d'ól ar cét longadh ocus ni dligheár atabhairt déis na coda oir adeir auicina sa caibidil cétna *Uinum post quodlibet omnium ciborum est malum* i is olc an fin taréis gach uile bídh ocus adir a caibidil follamhnuighthi an neith itter ocus ibhter *Uinum post cibum est ex rebus magis impedientibus digestionem* i dona neithibh is mó toirmisgius an dileaghadh fín d'ól taréis bídh arson cotabhair ar an mbiadh tolladh sul dileaghta e. *Et* ni himchubidh an fín ar in cuid doréir auicina sa caibidil labhrus d'follamhnughadh a neithe itter ocus ibhter mar an abair *Oportet ut post comestionem bibat quis et non in hora comedendi* is hégin gurob taréis an caithmhe ibhus nech deoch ocus nach an uair proindighti *Et* adeir began roimhe sin *Non est bibendum donec cibus de stomaco descendat* i ni dligheár deoch dh'ól no go tuitinn an biadh is an ghaile. *In opossitum* i ata in gnathughadh coitchind ina aguidh so ag ól an

Column VII.

an fin roimh an cuid an aimsir na sláinti Gidheadh is imchubidh e uait ann an aimsir na heslainti i intan is mó is egail uireasbhaidh na brígh na urchoid an fína mar is folluis isin t'singcoipis tig o anmhfainne na bríghi ocus adeirim gurub imchubidh e intan sin roimh in cuit ocus tai a héis Ocus intan doniter mar argamainti nach imchubaidh ar in cuid e adeirim doréir auicina sa caibidil labhrus d'follamhnughadh an uisgi ocus an fína nach urcoidigheann dá bhriala d'ól ar in cuid don nech dognathuigh e ocus mar in cétna don duine shlán déis cuislindi. Gidhegh dlighear an gnathughadh do coimeidh annso mad arrsaigh e muna fa ro-olc e ocus dleghai a treigen antan sin déis a céile ocus ni gohoband *Et* iseadh tuigim tiid in foculso briala i misun ina tuillfedh oirett éndighe amain i an méidh doghebadh nech gan claochlogh anala .i den anail gan coimhéigniughadh gan fostogh ainndeonach. Adeirim fós gurup olc an fín déis gach uile bídh acht taréis an bídh dobeith dileaghta ocus athuitme acht a *caninus apititus* mar an dlighear neithi meithi dotabhairt artús ocus fín aindsein ocus is dlighi leighis sin Gidhedh ni himchubaidh an fín déis bídh onginter droch leann na roimhe na intan caither e mar adeir auicina san inadh cétna oir doblur ar in droch linn sin tolladh cum foirimill an chuirp ocus is uime sin thsheacranaoid an drong lerbáil fín d'ól déis nan droch biadh dan dileaghadh ou imighi roimh in ndileaghadh ocus tromaighi an corp is uime sin adeirim gocumair gu féttar an fín dotabairt a méid big déis na coda ocus ni a caindigheecht móir ocus a tabairt do nech dognathuigh e ocus do neach déis cuislindi ocus gan a tabairt do neach eile acht an aimsir tharta móir ocus is na cásaibh eile curtur sa caibidil labrus d'follamhnughadh an uisgi ocus an fína. *Et* intan adeu nach imchubidh an fín ar in cuitt adeir-

Column VIII.

im gurob mar so dlighear briathra auicina dotuigsin antan adeir gurub taréis na coda dlighear an deoch d'ól ocus nach uirri .i. gurub taréis thsluigthi an grema ocus nach e trath ata sa bél dlighear a h'ól No(no)gan imurcraigh dh'ól antan caithius biadh ocus is ris sin adeir auicina caindighecht Is tarbhach don biadh nach dlighind nech d'ól ar in cuitt acht ni dobeiadh siubhal ar an mbiadh no gan ni do beradh siubhal ro-obond air d'ól no do denadh dealughadh atturia ocus an gaile no do beiadh ar snámh e. Gidhegh féttur began d'ól daéis indus gombiadh an biadh aina comusg ocus arna timprail gumaith ocus gan fundamint romór do denamh ocus gan móran do ól as a háithle acht na huaire d'imdughadh ocus gan an caindigheecht continoidech do méadughadh. *Et* is uime sin adeirim gofuilit tri deocha and i *Potus alteratiuus* i deoch claochluightech ocus *Potus permixtiuus* i deoch cumuisgthech ocus *Potus delatiuus* deoch imairctech An deoch claochluightech is roim an mbiadh is imchubidh i mar ataid na sirioipighi ocus na deocha leighis, ocus an deoch cumuisgtech is ar an cuid dlighear i ocus began do caithemh ocus began dól indus condernthar an cumusc dlistinech. An deoch imairctech, umorio, taréis na coda ocus ar ndenamh an dileaghtha ocus ar dtuitim an bídh as a gaile dlighear i no intan bhes ag a fágbhail *Et* is uíme sin adeir auerois sa dara paitegal do na cantigibh sa naoimhcadh comint fithed mar coisgius an t-uisge donttei a croccan fhuichach afiuchadh in t-uisgi no an deoch curthar acend an bídh bhis ag a dileaghadh sa gaile coisgidh an dileagha ocus is uime sin nach maith móran d'ól taréis na coda no combia in dileagha imslan sa gaile Acht is tarbhach cum an dileaghtha tart d'fhulang déis

.na coda. gidh ni hedir cāmaigth nanetic
ead issin tabhairta dfoillsiughadh o lettacaib
cindti mur adubairt .G. sa .3. paragraf do meg
athin mar dentur dofuith insa b3 fog
donfuilnim 7 daingniget dosh o ghibeta is
nite .III. 3. caibidil do no ridu · c · c · c ·

DOND INDIETA NO CAITME IN bidh

istriur .i. inntan eiriges neach 7 inuair issind
airtz .i. laimha 7 ainmnel 7 cuirp do a dangen go
glan uime 7 in darlaid aimsir inntinnigthecain
.c. oidhti 7 in .L. oidhti 7 in .3. oidhti leis eil 7 leth
innairecht nos ina 7 na bi iaighter oir is rud fos
airecta an .3. oidhti 7 an dosein comilead aneo
sis dambia aigh imeub aige arsson fuing
ill anallair 7 in luathaighi bisairintticinn
oir ata intticinn porisilmail 7 tabhraid cuig
gac ni bis angar do dosh .G. sa .c. leabur de
simplici medicinalis ann dosein ciridh
icind 7 in dul laimha 7 aaighaidh aluigh fuig
7 a tsamradh 7 aluighi ce sa geimridh 7 in
igeadh a sin li leluighi arna agimail sa
bel 7 arna teghadh ando 7 artuima ainneir
tamuige ando oir indaurb sin te ig narul
7 gabaid iat is comil aindsein a fuaclad
duill is iucaill isin tsamradh 7 lecicin ann
baill buidhe sa geimrid Isamdosein abuisi
actaimuir la ameili bz dil trag lis
tlrahaitlesin denadh sioctar 7 is iub ins
da aimsiraib ariuda glana 7 ullmaigt abi
adh indz dgalia biadh a.c. oir deir antro
tair sin intan tinsgnz a tochlugh go .n. 7 n
agab sonnie 7 na cuiredh a paill oir adh
aurta rucaibidil labhz do nuat 7 ibit go

tabhair fulang o caraius tar aghaidh angaile
do linadh do lenoib morguighe 7 ticann
sin linadh tadbair o .l. p. ar na tairruim
g cumbel angaile inoz sinedir anbiadh
do caithem lisin toc luig ainim de geimail
e 7 nolighean neac asait do caithem mara
dubimar soimain 7 miothin as enbiadh
do caithim ar .ondoro oir adauta san
inad e suas. Michil detepius quam ci
baria multiplicare 7 meis tlinpoz solon
gare .i. ni fuil nis measa na ta biada dind
ug 7 ainis dfagbaing aga caithim 7 is uime
sinad andernad caibidil se de regimine
cibi gurileor lis nas lucomib feoil aina
in do caithim samaid 7 gan ainim ara
suis 7 ni gabhdh oir biadh a examla antin
feidtt gidh da caithe biadh inda ar lue
iad isfeglir naneich, seime do tabhairt arz
7 naneich seimra aimsir na adaighidh a sin
oir intan caite inbiadh reim deis anbiadh
remhar doilgh golitte 7 in dentar anbiadh
seimhur 7 bidh se intan sin agairraid slug
eadh amac 7 ni fagann on biadh seimh dobi
ameice 7 tic de sin go comiris seire 7 go
taillt iule iat Is dead damb 7 afeis agne
ac in biadh do mizoing sirsingaile do biud
coir oirreat inmed is ced ici angaile na
anice dotabairt donbiadh seimhur arz
gidh inhedir l ni liza sin dodenaimo
nac flouriuis cadisnaidenta clon alec
naseime mar adir auicia a caibidil d'in
quartana 7 sa .x. paragraf do regimen
ta acutorum **IT** na gabadh biadh oing ·

COLUMN IX.

na coda gidhedh ni héidir caindigheeht na neithead is intabhurta d'foillsiughadh o leitreachuibh cindti mar a deir g[alen] sa treas partegul do megathegni inaseadh dentur doréir mhesa bus fogus don fhírindi ocus daingnighter doréir dherbhtha ocus gnathuighthi e In treas caibidil don Ord

D'Órd in Dieta no Caithmc in Bhidh—is e so e i intan éireochas neach sa mhaidin sínedh artús a lamha ocus a mhuinel ocus cuiredh aedaighi go glan uime ocus indarbadh ainnsein imurcracha in cét dileaghtha ocus in dara dileagha ocus in treas dileaghtha le seiledh ocus le himurcrachaib na sróna ocus na bráighedh oir is iad so imarcracha an treas dileaghtha ocus aindsein coimleadh an corp dambia aimsir imcubidh aige arson fhuighill an alluis ocus in luaithrigh bis air in croicind oir ata in croicinn poiremhail ocus tairngidh cuigi gach ní bis angar dó doréir g[alen] sa cét leabur *de simplici medicina.* *Et* aindsein círeadh a chend ocus indladh a lamha ocus a aighiadh a huisgi fhuai sa t'shamradh ocus a huisgi the sa geimhregh ocus nigheadh a shúili le huisglii arna congmhail sa bhél ocus arna theghadh and ocus ar tuma an méir tanuisti and oir indurbidh sin tursgar na súl ocus glanaidh iat *Et* coimleadh aindhsein a fhiacla le duille ureuill isin t'samhradh ocus le croicinn an ubhaill buidhe sa geimhredh *Et* aindsein aburadh a trátha muiri no a ní eili bhus dúthracht lis As a h'aithle sin denadh saothar ocus siubhal mesarrdha an inaduibh árda glana ocus ullmuigter a biadh indus congabha biadh a cét oir déis an thsaothair sin intan tinnsgnus a thochlugadh go nadurdha ocus na gabhadh roimhe ocus na cuireadh afaill oir adeir auicina sa caibidil labhrus doní ithter ocus ibhter go

COLUMN X

tabair fulang ocaruis tar a gnathughadh angaili do línadh do lenduibh morguighthi ocus tic antan sin línadh tadhbais o lind ruadh arna tarruing cum béil an ghaili indus nach éidir an biadh do caithim lis in thochlugadh ainmhidhe go madh áil e ocus ni dlighcann neach a sháith docaitimh mar adubhramar roimhainn ocus ni dlighinn acht énbhiadh do caithimh ar aon bórd oir adeir auicina san inadh th'shuas *Nichil deterius quam cibaria multiplicare et in eis temporibus prolongare* .i. ni fuil ní is measa na na biadha d'imdhughadh ocus aimsir d'faidiughadh ag a caithimh ocus is uime sin adeir an deiradh caibidilech *de regimine cibi* gur leór lis na sendaoinibh feoil amhain do caithimh sa maidin ocus aran amhain ar a suiper ocus ni gabdhaois biadha examhla an éinfheacht Gidhedh da caithter biadh imdha ar énchuid is ferr na neithi seimhe dotabairt artús ocus na neithi remhia ainnsein na a contraida sin oir intan caithter in biadh seimh déis an biadh remair diligher goluath e ocus ni dentai an biadh remhur ocus bidh se intan sin ag iarnaidh slighcadh amach ocus ni fhaghann on biadh remhar do beith an íchtar ocus tic de sin go comuisgter ris e ocus go truaillter uile iat Gidheadh dambeith a fhis ag neach in biadh do meadughadh iis in ghaili do budh cóir oireat in méid is teo íchtar an ghaili na a uachtai dotabairt don biadh remhur artús Gidhedh ni héidir no ni h'urusa sin do denamh ocus o nach féduruis cad is indenta claon aleith na seimhe mar adir auicina a caibidil leighis in quartana ocus sa dara partegul do *regimenta acutorum* *Item* na gabhadh biadh omh ar

Column XI

muin bídh leth bruithi *Et* dlighear a fis uime sin gombi in biadh a comnuighi sa corp sul dilighthar go himlan e sea huair dég mai adeir aueroys sa dara partegul do na canticibh ocus adeirai in cétna sa caibidil deighinuigh don tseiseadh leabhuir do colliget go ataid naoi nuaire ag a radh a leabhraibh éigin ocus is brég sin oir is dóigh gurub e in sgribneoir fuair nuimir éigin sgribhtha ocus ni fitter catt í ocus do rinn e seachran ag sgribhadh ocus is sea huairi dég do dhlighfeadh beith and ocus is e a cúis sin oir adeir auicina a caibidil *de regimine cibi* ocus aueroes isna canticibh gurub e is proindiughadh orduighthi ann biadh do caithimh fathrí sa dá la i fadhó ládibh ocus einfecht lá eile ocus dlighith sea huaire dég beith ittir gach dá uair dibh sin indus go roindfigter in dá lá nadurda ina fuilitt ocht nuaire ocus dá fithet go comtiom a trí rannuibh ocus is e a adhbur sin madho rindeadh sechtan sa ló inaicaith fadhó go certuighter e arnamhárach ag caithimh énuair ocus *e contrario* oir gach olc doniter on linadh leighisigh in folmughadh e ocus *e contrario* mar adeirar sa dara partegul d'*aforismorum* Gidheadh adeir auicina sa treas leabur sa treas fén dég sa treas trachtadh ocus sa caibidil labrus do moille tuirlingha an bliadh asa ghaili *Remanencia equalis cibi in stomacho et egressionis eius est illud quod est inter duodecim horas et uiginti duas* i isi aimsir cuttroma anmhana in bídh isin gaili ocus a fhagbala dhó ambi ittir da uair dég ocus a dhó fithteat tre moilli oiprighthi na brighi dileaghthaighi ocus is uime sin adeirim othcid an biadh go remar isin gaili gurub sia anus and na inaduibh nan dileaghadh eili oir is seimhe in chilus na in t'aian ocus is uime sin is luath inntaighter a fuil deirg e ocus is luath indtaighter fuil derg aros a póiribh nam ball ocus tic lis in radh so auicina in biadh do dhileaghadh

Column XII

isna ballaibh uili re sea huairibh dég go teagmadh gan a cur a cosmailius gohuilidhi rui isin fedh sin gidheadh anuidh uair and o anmhfainne an ghaile ocus o reimhe ocus o righne an bídh re ocht nuairibh dég no ré fitit uair sa gaili mai is follus a neimhdhileaghadh an gaili ocus intan caithius nech biadha urchoideacha eigin anus uair and a póiribh an ghaili ré mí no ré ráithi mar do chuala o daoinib fírindecha gur sgeigheadur bídh ocus leighes uair éigin sa cainndighecht ocus sa t'substaint mar gabattar iat mí roime sin. Tuilleadh eile dlighear d'foillsiughadh i nach imcubidh baindi ocus iasg ai én bórd na fín ocus baindi oir ullmuighit nech cum lúbra ocus na gabhthur lictuairi iotesaigi déis an bhídh goluath na énní diureticeach oir truaillitt an biadh aga losgadh no aga chur ar siubhul go roluath ocus is uime sin is olc in drageta do níter do maratrum ocus d'anís cona cosmuilibh goluath déis na coda oir is ferr cumsanadh ina sesamh no siubul ailginach do denamh déis in bídh mai a dubhuirt rufhus *Modicus incessus post prandium hoc est quod michi placet* i is mian liumsa began siubhuil taréis na coda gidheadh gluasacht mór do denamh deis in proindighthi dosiubul no do marchuideacht truaillidh in biadh ocus toirmisgidh an dileaghadh Ashaithli sin codladh go mesarrdha oir furtachtaighi sin in dileaghadh mar adeirur sa canoinsi *Uentres hieme et uere* gurub maith rena thuigsin a méd fhuirtachtaighius in codladh in dileaghadh gidheadh is olc in codladh ocus in nemh-codladh téid tar modh amach mai adeirur sa dara partegul d'*aforismorum* ocus dentar e san oidhci oir adeir ip[ocras] sa cét partegul do *pronosticorum Sompnus naturnalis est qui noctem non effugit et*

mun bid l. brisid [illegible] aspis uime [illegible]
gombi in bid a comhmilis [illegible] a co[illegible]
[illegible] go himlane o [illegible] maraid [illegible]
[illegible] dona cinticib [illegible]
c. [illegible] acubidil [illegible] don. o [illegible]
do colliget [illegible] a tamd [illegible] mair [illegible]
ale abrlaib [illegible] brig [illegible]
[illegible] inis [illegible] mainmuinis [illegible]
in [illegible] cant [illegible]
[illegible] o [illegible] do olis [illegible]
ano [illegible] a cuir [illegible] ad aucta acaibid
il [illegible] cibi [illegible] nacait
icib [illegible] anbiad
do [illegible] sa dala [illegible] laoib [illegible]
la [illegible] o [illegible] da
[illegible] insula
[illegible] g. [illegible]
a z. [illegible]
[illegible] inaiceat [illegible]
[illegible] ag [illegible]
ole [illegible] inolme [illegible]
mar [illegible] sa. x. [illegible] morum
[illegible] ad aucta sa z. [illegible]
[illegible] incaibidil [illegible]
plinga anbiaid a [illegible] Remanmuncia ex
malis cibi in stomacho [illegible] eius
illud quod [illegible]
[illegible] anman
anbid [illegible] da
[illegible]
[illegible] anbiad go
[illegible]
[illegible] inchib [illegible]
[illegible]
[illegible]
[illegible] anbiad do [illegible]

[illegible] o [illegible]
gan a cuir a corp [illegible]
[illegible] o anmpainn [illegible]
[illegible] anbid [illegible] g [illegible]
[illegible] mair [illegible]
[illegible]
[illegible] a [illegible]
[illegible]
[illegible] bid [illegible]
[illegible] subsistunt [illegible]
[illegible]
[illegible]
[illegible] cumlubra [illegible]
[illegible] anbiad
go luat [illegible] each [illegible]
[illegible]
[illegible] ole [illegible]
[illegible] mullach
[illegible] na coda [illegible]
[illegible] no [illegible]
[illegible] mar [illegible] doig
incessus post prandium hoc est quod
michi placet. [illegible] linum [illegible]
[illegible] na coda [illegible]
[illegible] no dong
[illegible] anbiad [illegible] an
[illegible] cool [illegible]
[illegible] mar [illegible]
[illegible] hieme [illegible]
[illegible] in
cool [illegible] ole incool [illegible]
[illegible] cool [illegible] mar [illegible]
[illegible] morum [illegible]
[illegible]
[illegible] na
[illegible] quia noctem non [illegible]

diem non impedit .i. is ⁊ codl. .ii. ann in
codl. nach fuair indoidchi ⁊ nach toirmisgi
na inla giolg donit dcoimet imda ladon
oidchi ag codl. ⁊ a lo ⁊ ma ndentar ni
dci ⁊ is ro olc sin giolg. ol. tu a fir gnib
ar in taobh nolis ol. codl. ar ts oiris
maisin is fearr donit an oil ad arson
nan le do b⁊ fo i ingaili ann ⁊ oil ar im
pog ar in taobh cle ar a haithli ach tiugst
an biadh cumnaige sul oil e go linmlis
impog ar is quin taobh noltas ing gunadh
usaide taisbongt. ann do oil ad sagai
li cumnaige ⁊ tuict. ro aca sa cai
bidil labr. o follamhnug ann tic ⁊ ibt
sa caibidil labrus don codl. ⁊ don nlsinco
ol ⁊ ad fos ann sin go tabhaid tindsgain
c loig arinnim don fortacht mor cum
an doilta arson go inman antl. n. ⁊ gu
ta ermaingindi e gib iuimt sin mednig
e giolg is olc codl. faoi ⁊ is olc don
fearr codl. go lur doir bid ⁊ is olc fos
codl. le munaoid angar doberr aru
ig e ⁊ ataig mait dir na coda ⁊ isin
tramsi ⁊ brean in tan sin fos ⁊ is iuim
e sin ad in fearaistoir. Aut breuis aut
nullus sit sompnus meridianus .i. bit
codl. in meadoin lae gearr no na dentar e
gidhedh dandentar noim incuit e orm
e omhaidin go ccs dor .i. r. sa. t. paricis
dopprometticorum Q ingaibt adeirit
⁊ in blel oslurg. arsgla oc ceir doaid
ast tac do toirmesgadh inoil ⁊ bit in
clind go hard isin codl. ⁊ cluit le hed
go mait e dor aurta ⁊ is ro mait sin cail
indoilta. Sit meas puuig. aicioig nah
an ma ⁊ is iuime sin ad in fearaistoir
Sit tibi mensis lecta labor ⁊ modo
rata dieta .i. bit mensima t. uilb

agat ⁊ diet in sorda ⁊ oirnas coit fa
si mor fogius fot. gadh iusgimilis .s.
n. bia biad isingaile & bit insin uperi
gear no ed.m muna bia in ngnatug ing
aigid oir do leit indoilta donit isin
codl. do biud fearr nibiud mo do biad doc
aitiun is noidci giolg. odomit in codl. go
poluat fulcontis anbiadh obel ingaili
is iuime sin is ro mor usicoiduigius
moran in badh s anoidce don fiadh ursc
⁊ is iuime sin atait moran o fear taobh
ar annta sa. Nocturna cena fit
stomaco maxima pena .i. is mor a
pian do goile suipeir na hoidce
Ut sis esse leuis sit tibi cena breuis
madh mail leat b ⁊ eorum biot dosnip
co gear ⁊ ata da fearr a ele ar an .ca.
Cena breuis uel cena leuis fit raro
molesta .i. is annam is ait uulta an
suipeir gearr no eorum Magna
nocet medicina docet. res e. man
efesta .i. teagasgthug an ealadha leigis
⁊ is ro mo follus comaicoidim ar suip
mor tuill fos. Sume cibum modice
modico natura souetur .i. cait beagan bi
d oir sastar in .ii. obl. an Sic corpus p
efice ne mens ieiuna grauetur
.i. suipeib amhl. sasfaidhe an corp ⁊ gan
tsuime do bi ⁊ aran intinn i ocsfig
innsead tabuirt an biadh uait ing
is tusga toct. an n. e. Fit in oriens
an fual ⁊ an fearadh ⁊ fuscaite ar
en corp ma tarlamuinn ar ainocait
an innaithib oir do gelnaoir duinte
is ina tcobainb ⁊ is ainsanac is na clua
saib oir go tochmuis ag impog ru
is no cloc no ysoopus ocogbail ar
fuail sin o atom ocod ocliracint

Column XIII

diem non impedit .i is sin is codladh nadurda and in codladh nach sechnann in oidchi ocus nach toirmisgind in lá. Gidhegh doint daoine imdha lá don oidchi ag codladh sa ló ocus ina ndúsacht san oidchi ocus is ro-olc sin. Gidhegh dlighidh tu atis gurub ar in taobh ndes dlighear codladh artús oir is mar sin is ferr do niter an dileaghadh arson nan ae do beith faoi in gaili and ocus dlighur impog ar in taobh clé asaháithli conach tairngter an biadh cum nan ae sul dlightur gohimli e ocus impogh arís ar in taobh ndeas innus gumadh usaide tarrongtar an ní do dileaghadh sa ghaili cum nan ae ocus tuicter so o auicina sa caibidil labrus d'follamnughadh aneith itter ocus ibter ocus isa caibidil labhrus don codladh ocus don nemh-codladh ocus aden fós and sin go tabhair tindsgaint loighi ar in medon furtacht mór cum an dileaghtha arson go connmhann an tes nadurda ocus gu tachmaingind e gurub uime sin méduigter e. Gidhegh is olc codladh faon ocus is olc don radarc codladh goluath déis bídh ocus is olc fós codladh lae muna dernter angar do beith asuighi e ocus athaigh maith déis na coda ocus isin th'samradh ocus becan intan sin fós ocus is uime sin adeir in fersaighteoir *Aut breuis aut nullus sit somnus meridianus* i bith codladh in meadoin-lae gerr no na dentur e Gideagh dan derntur roimh in cuit e dentur o mhaidin go teirt doréir ip[ocrais] sa dara partegul do *pronosticorum*. *Et* ingaibhter a dhenumh ocus in bél osluigthi aregla droch aeir do dul asteach do toirmeosgadh in dileaghadh ocus bith in cend gohárd isin chodladh ocus cluthur le hédach gomaith e do réir auicina ocus is ro-maith sin cum in dileaghtha. *Item* measruighter aicidigi na hanma ocus is uime sin adeir in fersaightheoir *Sit tibi mens leta labor et moderata dieta* i. bith menma tshuilbir

Column XIV.

agat ocus diet mesurdha ocus déna saotar *Et* is mor fhoghnus fothrugadh uisgi milis acht nach bia biadh isin gaile *Et* bith in super gerr no édrom muna bia in gnathughadh ina aighidh oir do leith in dileaghtha do niter isin codladh do budh ferr ni budh mhó do biadh do caithimh isin oidchi gidhegh o doniter in codladh go ro-luath sul toitis an biadh o bél in ghaili is uime sin is ro-mór urchoidighius móran in bidh san oidche don radhurc ocus is uime sin ataitt móran d'fersadhaibh ar an adhbarsa *Nocturna cena fit stomaco maxima pena* i is mór an pian do goile super na h'oidhce *Si uis esse leuis sit tibi cena breuis* madháil let bheith édrum bioth do shuiper cogerr ocus ata dá fersa ele ar an cétna *Scena breuis uel cena leuis raro molesta* i is andam is athuimulta an suiper gearr no édrum *Magna nocet medicina docet res est manefesta* i teagasgaigh an caladha leighis ocus is raod fholluis con urcoididhinn an suipei mór Tuilleadh fós *Sume cibum modice modico natura foueatur* i caith began bidh oir sástur in nadur o began *Sic corpus refice ne mens urina grauetur* gurub amlaidhi shásfaidhter an corp gan truime do bheith ar an menmuin on trégenus maseadh tabuir an biadh uait mar is tusga tochluighes an nadur e *Item* indarbtur an fual ocus in feradh ocus na fastaighter ar éncor iad tar an aimsir a san dtaighter an indharbadh oir do gendaois duinte isna taobhaibh ocus siansanach isna cluasaibh on gaothmuirecht ag impogh suas no cloch no ydoripis o chongbail an fuail Sin duit a eoin o aodh o cendainn

COLUMN XV.

Nec minctum retinere uelis nech cogere uentrem .i narub ál let th'fual do congmail na do meadhon d'éigniughadh i tar an aimsir ina beitter gomaith e ocus is uime sin nach maith beith gu ro-fadha ar in camra na fásgadh éigneach do denamh ocus is uime sin is sea huaire is maith in fual do tabairt sa ló conoidchi oir is e sin in lá nadurda ocus in feradh fadhó no fathrí san aimsir cétna mar adeirit na ferrsadh so *In die minctura fit sexies naturali tempore bis tali uel ter sit egestio pura* .i in cetruma caibidil don aimsir

Don aimsir i dleghur aimsir na bliadhna do féchuin oir is cóir ni éigin do tabairt d'aire do leith na haoisi ocus in fhuind ocus na h'aimsiri mar adeirur sa chéd partegul, d'*aforismorum* Maseadh tabuirtur biadh iemur a méid móir sa gheimredh on adirur san madh cétna *Uentres hieme et uere calulissimi sunt natura* i ataid na cabain inmedhonach ro-the doréir nadura sa geimredh ocus san errach ocus bidh in codladh ro-fhada gurb uime [sin] dlighear móran in bidh do tabuirt ocus ni dlighear na proinndighi dobeith minic oi ni bfuil an tes gear[i] ann mar bis san tsamhradh acht mór doréir shínti tre imad na spirut Gidhegh bidh in tes beg isin tsamradh a gabail thesa arson cuirp the nis sa mó doréir shínte an édluis no in disgaoilti ocus ni doréir shínte na caimndigheachta acht doréir ainde ocus dlighi an biadh bheith a claonadh cum tesa antansin ocus is folluis as sin cred is inraidh re tes nan daoine óg ocus na macam

San earrach, umorro, dlighear an biadh bheith mesurrdha acht a claonadh cum méide bige arson an línta do rinnedh sa geimredh roimhe.

Sa tsamhradh, umorro, dlighi an biadh bheith seimh

COLUMN XVI

ag dul a bfuaire ocus is seimh ina caimndighecht sin i began do tabhairt an éinecht de oir bidh substaint in tesa beg intan sin arna cnaoi ocus arna disgaoileadh on tes foirimeallach ocus da tucaoi biad seimh ina shubstaint do loisgfidhe on tes teinntighe e ocus is uime [sin] adeir g[alen] sa canoinsí *Uentres hieme et cetera* go téid an tes a bfoinnill sa tsamradh agabail luthgaire re na cosmailius gurub uime sin anbfuinnighter go hinnmeonach e San bfoghmair, umorro, tabhair an biadh a geaimndighecht big ocus dlighi beith ag dul a tesoighecht ocus a bflichidacht ocus ataid fersadha air so *Quantum uis sume de mensa tempore brune* caith an mhéid is ál leat don biadh an aimsir in geimridh *Tempore sed ueris cibo moderate frueris* gnathaigh biadh go mesurrdha an aimsir an erraich. *Et calor estatis dapibus nocet in moderatis* do ní tes an tsamraidh urchoid do na biadoibh mí-mesurrdha *Autumpni fructus extremos dant tibi luctus* do beird toirthi an foghmhair caoinedh dermair duit.

In cuigeadh caibidil—d'uairib in proinnighthi. Is i uair in proinnighthi antan bhis an t'ocarus fírinneach ann mar adubhramar sa treas caibidil t'suas ocus is i uair is fearr sa tsamradh an uair is fuaire i roimh an teirt ocus an uair na hespartan ocus isi uair an éigentuis intan is éider le nech biadh d'faghbhail ocus is uime sin adeir g[alen] *in libro de regemine sanitatis* nach eidir le nech d'follamnachu na slainti do congmail acht a nech bes gan toirmisg o aon gnodugh

Bec mistaim pretinere uelis nec co
gere uentrem .i. [illegible] fual
do congmail [illegible] dergnius .i.
[illegible] gonaic [illegible]
[illegible] mac [illegible] fada [illegible]
caimpa na [illegible] fignac [illegible]
[illegible] is mait [illegible]
fual do tibairt [illegible] ise
[illegible] .ii. [illegible] fada nofa .z. [illegible]
[illegible] .c. [illegible] adeit [illegible]

Poie minctura fit series nactura
In Tempore bisextali uel ceterisque egest
io. purga .i. in [illegible] cabtoil [illegible]
Don aimsir .i. [illegible] inablia [illegible]
[illegible] is coir [illegible] do tab. [illegible]
dolei [illegible] mal [illegible] inaiaimsir in
ar [illegible] ceo [illegible]
[illegible] tabairt [illegible]
[illegible]
[illegible] .c. m. uentres [illegible] cuilo
[illegible] sunt [illegible] .i. [illegible]
[illegible] doq. ii. [illegible]
[illegible] incod [illegible]
[illegible] do tabairt [illegible]
[illegible]
[illegible]
[illegible]
[illegible]
[illegible]
[illegible]
[illegible]
[illegible]
[illegible]
[illegible]
Sanguis [illegible]
[illegible]
[illegible]
S [illegible]

[illegible]
[illegible]
[illegible]
[illegible]
[illegible]
[illegible]
[illegible]
[illegible]
[illegible]
[illegible]
[illegible]
[illegible] S [illegible]
[illegible]
[illegible]
[illegible]
[illegible]
[illegible] Tempore [illegible]
[illegible]
[illegible]
[illegible] Et [illegible]
[illegible] nocet in modernis [illegible]
[illegible]
[illegible]
[illegible]
[illegible]
[illegible]

In .ii. caibid [illegible]

Sinus [illegible]
[illegible]
[illegible] .z. caibidil [illegible]
[illegible]
[illegible]
[illegible]
[illegible]
[illegible]
[illegible]
[illegible]
[illegible]

[illegible] gle ⁊ [illegible] ⁊ [illegible]
[illegible] [illegible] .u.c.
[illegible] [illegible] ⁊ [illegible] .c.
[illegible] ⁊ [illegible]
[illegible] ⁊ [illegible]
[illegible]
[illegible] ⁊ [illegible]
[illegible] ⁊ [illegible]
[illegible]
.i. d. caibid do gnaich

D lesair gnaitis indiscail do [illegible]
[illegible] olc ⁊ [illegible]
[illegible] go mill ⁊ is [illegible]
in gnaich [illegible] les [illegible]
[illegible] mail ⁊ [illegible]
[illegible] mail for
[illegible]
[illegible] ⁊ ni [illegible]
[illegible]
[illegible]
go [illegible]
[illegible] for [illegible]
⁊ is [illegible]
[illegible] go minic
⁊ minic [illegible] cabr
[illegible] oir [illegible]
[illegible] dia [illegible] ingac
[illegible] .a.c. oir [illegible]
[illegible] ⁊ [illegible] ⁊ [illegible]
in .ii. uile .i. [illegible] aca
[illegible]
on [illegible] .a.c. [illegible]
[illegible] bid [illegible]
[illegible] ni [illegible]
do [illegible] gle ⁊ is [illegible]
[illegible] gle [illegible]

[illegible]
[illegible]
[illegible]
[illegible] luc[illegible] [illegible] ⁊ [illegible]
[illegible] ⁊ [illegible]
[illegible]
.i. ⁊ [illegible] oir [illegible]
[illegible] dib [illegible]
oir is [illegible] na [illegible]
[illegible] ⁊ is [illegible] [illegible]
[illegible] ⁊ [illegible] ⁊ [illegible]
[illegible] is [illegible] in [illegible]
[illegible] ingabail mar ad graacitor
tis particularibus glosu
atain gnitur coitcind iaa
ig fo guhele oir domitrod
[illegible] ⁊ is [illegible]
[illegible] a caitim mailt [illegible] oir
cathid ne gaciuli [illegible]
[illegible] glosois
[illegible] ⁊ is [illegible]
[illegible] follaim [illegible]
[illegible] .c. [illegible]
[illegible]
bid [illegible] le [illegible]
[illegible]
[illegible] ⁊ [illegible] ⁊ [illegible]
[illegible] ⁊ [illegible]
⁊ is [illegible] Qui [illegible]
et mulierem [illegible] in corde [illegible]
[illegible]
[illegible] na [illegible] ⁊
[illegible] ⁊ [illegible]
[illegible]
[illegible] gle [illegible]
[illegible] ⁊ is [illegible] gle [illegible]

Column XVII.

igentach eile air ocus ag ambeit a chuingill saor in gach énní Sa geimhredh, imorro, toghthar in uair bhus teo ocus mar an cétna don eriach ocus don foghmhar oi annchuidid ris in samradh ocus reis an geimhredh oir as annsna rannuibh is nesa don samhradh dibh dlighid in uair bheith mar uair an tsamhraidh ocus is na rannoibh is nesa don geimredh toghthar in uair bhus teo mesurrda

In seiseadha caibidil—don ghnathughadh Dlegar gnathugh in dieta do congmail nuna ba ro-olc e ocus madegh dlighear a treigen go mall ocus is uime sin in gnathughadh aontuighius leis na neithi nadurda dlighear a congmail ocus da tosgaigh e egan uatha dlighear a chongmail fós Gidegh mad mór in tosgaghadh dlighear a reorughadh tar a ais ocus ni gohobonn mar adubrumar Gidhegh tabhradh lucht an droch fhollamhnuighthi anair riu oir gin gon airgid ar an lathair e aireochuid fós go-naith mar adeir auicina ocus is uime sin an drong adeir gur línadar iad fein do biadh go minic ocus nach derrna én urchoid doibh tabhradh an aire riu oir goirteochar iad oi a ndernadh dia dighultus in gach én pecadh a cét oir déis a dhénta ni bheith duine na bethaidh ocus mar ata in nadur uilidh i dia is mar sin ata a náduir rannaighthi sa duine nach dénonn dighultus a cét oi acht a gcinn aimsire *Item* bidh drong ann haitheas nisa mó do thorrthuibh na do biadhaibh eile ocus is sechranach do níd sin ir doni gach uile thoradh fuil

Column XVIII

isgemail mítarbhach somorgtha Gidheagh dlighear torrtha stipeghdha do haithemh déis an bídh dambia an medon lactach mar ataid péiredha ocus coctana ocus úbhla. Gidhedh lagaid na húbla rósdaighthi roim an chuid lucht lenna ruaidh ocus istipeda na húbla omha ocus ni comói ata gach gné dibh mar sin oir is lugha stipeda na húbla millsi ocus is mó na húbla goirti Na bolais, imorro, ocus na isineadha ocus na figedha is roim in cuid dlighur an gabhail mar adeir Ysaac *in dietis particularibus* Gidhedh ata in gnathughadh coitcind ina aighidh so gu h'olc oir donit so uinti ona neithi ocus is uime sin dlighear a caithimh maille sinnsi oir cathaighidh re ach uili truailleadh tic ona torthuibh doréir auicina Gidhedh is ferr na toirthi uile o tregin ocus is uime sin innisis g[alen] a leabur follamhnaighti na slainti goiaibhi a thair fén cét bliadhan ina bhethaidh arson nar chaith toirrthi *Item*, bidh drong ann a nab inmain irboill nan ainmintigh nisa mó na an chuid ele ocus drong ele a gcinn ocus drong ele a a genamha ocus mar sin do na ballaibh ele Ocus is uime sin adeir n fersaso *Pisces et mulieres sunt in caudis meliores uel dulciores* is inan errannaibh is ferr o is millsi na héisg ocus na mná ocus ni bfuil ann sin ac gurub lugha is fuar in tiasg naherr arson in gluasachta na sa cuid eile dhe Gidhedh is usa na boill eile do dileaghadh

COLUMN XIX.

mur ıs follus dotharr ın bradaın ocus da cosmaılıbh. Gıdhedh ısı ın cuıd ıs mó bıs ar gluasacht ıs lugha ımurcacha ocus ıs uime sın ıs ı ıs ferr ısna haınmınnthıbh caıthıd na daıno dambıa cudrumacht rıa ısna neıthıbh elı. Maseadh toghtar ın cuıdh ıs maeıthı ocus bıs ar gluasacht hegın ocus bus fearr blas oır ıs e ın ní ıs fearr blas ıs ferr oılus dambıa cudrumacht elı ann Gıdhedh adeır ın feısa *Non ualet ın ıccore quod dulce scıt ın oıre* ı nı maıth ıs na haeıbh ın ní ıs mılıs ısın bel. Ocus is don mılsi aenda tuıghter sın. Gıdhedh adeırım do na cnoıb and so nachfuıl etır nahuılı toradh déıs na fígeadh ocus na rísınedh toradh ıs ferr na ıad ocus ıs uime sın adeır ın fersa *Dıc auellanas epatı semper fore sanas* .ı abaır gurab fallaın na cnó do sír do na haeıbh. Tuılleadh elı, adeırim .i an drong leıbáıl coımrıachtachaın do gnathughadh nach dlıghıd a denam ocus a meadhon lán ach ar críchnughadh ın cét dıleaghtha ocus ın dara dıleaghtha ocus leıthı ın treas dıleaghtha ocus g(a)na a denumh gomınıc oir anmfaınnıghı sın go mói an gaılı ocus ın corp uılı ocus ıs ro-mór urcoıdıghıus don radhurc oır cuırıdh na súıle an doımne ro-

COLUMN XX.

-móır go follus Don cuıslınd, umorro, dlıghear a fis nach maıth a ro-gnathughadh oır adeır auıcına a caıbıdıl na cuıslınne co cúısıghınd an cuıslınn romınc aphoplexıa ocus adeır g[alen] sa naoımeadh leabhur do meghathegnı *Mınucıo ceterıs euacuacıonıbus uırtutı maıorem debılıtatem ınfert* ıse folmughadh na cuıslınde ıs mó anmfaınnıghıus an brígh de na huılıdh fholmughadh ocus as se adhbhur sın gurob mó ıs cara don nádur fuıl derg naıd leanda ele ocus ıs uime sın ıs e a folmughadh antan ıs ımurcach e ıs mó anbhaınnighıus munabia an duıne óg ocus complex fola deırge aıge ocus e a cumsanadh ocus a gnathughadh dh'feoil ocus do bıadhuıbh eıle oılıus comaıth oır dlıghıtt sın ar egla squınancıa ocus nescoıdedh ınmedonach cuıslı doleıgen nıs mınıca na nech eıle Et dlıghear rıaghaıl do bir damasenus sa dara paıtegul do *afoırısmorum* fein sa naoıneadh comınt ocus dá fıthett do congmaıl .ı. mad do gnathuıgh nech ına oıge cuıslı dolıgen fa cheıthır sa blıadhaın nach dlıghınd a lıgen acht fathrí acınd dara fithett blıadhan ocus én uaır amhaın acınd a trı fıthıtt blıadhan ocus o chınd a deıch ocus trí fıthıtt no ceathra fıthıtt blıadhan gan a lıgen go huılıdhı Gıdhedh as ı medıana dlıghear do lıgen acınd trı fithitt blıadhan ocus basılıca acınd dá fıthett blıadhan oır nı cóır cefalıca

muir is follus do tair in bradan
7 da cosmail gid 7 is incuid is m
o bis ar gluas- is luga immircach
7 is uaime fri [illegible] is fir is na liaaimsir
tib caitid nadaine dambia cu
[illegible] mair is nairib eli mast
ogtair incuid is inacht 7 bis air
gluas- [illegible] fraisi blas
airi [illegible] blas is frisi oilis
dambia cudrumus eli an gid 7 ad
infra Non ualet inter corpe qu
od dulce sed moise .i. innait
is na liaib inis imbis in bel 7 is
don millsi [illegible] da tuige fri n gid 7
adim don a chnoib [illegible] nac fuil
[illegible] na luili coir deis na figead 7
nair fed coir is fris na iad 7 is
uime fri ad infra Dic auellan
as spacii temporis forte sanas
.i. abair gur ab fuillan na cnodori
donaliaib Tuill eli adum .i. a
ding lesbail commuasasai
gnatuig nac oligid adennan 7
anneadon lan ac ar cenuig in
.c. ditta 7 in darna dilta 7 leith 7
.3. dilta 7 gna adennuin gomi
ic oir anfaaimsi fri gomora
gail 7 in corp uili 7 is romor
ucoraig dona adaigib oire
[illegible] na ruile an doinine ro

moir gofollus Non circius lind .u.
ol [illegible] orr .ad. .uii.
acanbrioil [illegible] cocuma [illegible] an
[illegible] apoplexia 7 ad. [illegible] ra
[illegible] leabair [illegible]
Diminucio ceterus euacuacionibus
[illegible] debilitate inplaut: is e
folmugad na [illegible] is mo [illegible]
[illegible] folmuga 7 [illegible]
[illegible] gobmo is [illegible]
[illegible] ele 7 is [illegible]
is e a folmugad [illegible] is [illegible]
e is mo [illegible] mununa bia [illegible]
[illegible] og 7 comnol [illegible] 7 e
[illegible] 7 a [illegible] 7 dob
[illegible] eile [illegible] comnart [illegible] dligit
fri [illegible] sequirancia 7 [illegible]
in imbodh [illegible] do leigin [illegible] minica
manlech ele [illegible] do bir [illegible]
[illegible] pairt [illegible] do [illegible]
feirsas comnirt 7 [illegible] do con
gm. .i. [illegible]
do ligin fa [illegible] rabtain [illegible] a ligin
[illegible] fa .3. acind .2. [illegible] blian 7 [illegible]
[illegible] acind a .3. [illegible] blian [illegible]
cind a deich 7 .3. [illegible] no [illegible]
blian gan a ligin go [illegible]
[illegible] do ligin acind [illegible]
[illegible] blian 7 basilica acind [illegible]
[illegible] blian oir ni coir cefalica

do ligin ocind da ptla blian anaic
oir dall ⁊ rl. ⁊ Uillt mc uimint
Uair tog moi nabla .ii. cunnacht
rthi .i. int Ghrac ⁊ in fogmuir giold
ni cuirle an Ghriug is fgir aid oir
impuil enim comitt nle airirt ibi in
tri[illegible]ig mar doni cuirli an Ghriug
dofi aniuca giorad is an duramuil fod
mile aimsir nabla uili dosi na tucad
.i. airimit ad ⁊ angeimin [illegible] ollt
in cuirli doligin anaimsir nofuair in
nocte ⁊ is uinnt is is coit clst [illegible] uall
mug inord leir bail cuirli doligin
uinfeil scefain ⁊ uinfeil eoin baist
t fuair aimsir dib ⁊ t cli nahaim
ri eli r golig uair ano uinn nodlug
i dochraig q nahirt ibi dogenteoi onl
mad guach dodenam acoitcint is an
Don teob arand olt aligin ... ad insgaig
Cuir Ketar uer dextr autumpnizem
pisque [illegible] .i. nalama [illegible]
n Ghrac ⁊ [illegible] ⁊ nalama cle [illegible]
fogmuir ⁊ [illegible] dol ⁊ [illegible]
[illegible] luna uetz uectis iuuentis noue
luna [illegible] .i. ali[illegible] dona [illegible] com
ib intan is airriug [illegible] ⁊ dona dcom
ib [illegible] intan is nua Don [illegible] daith
na cuirlindi olt [illegible] doent r [illegible]
oir and sin oir bit dcoint an lebail mor
an dol ⁊ dith intan sin dogeinlmuin
fola [illegible] cadfa [illegible] ⁊ is [illegible]
sin dligit bl [illegible] an dol ⁊ dith giold ol
[illegible] nis mo dol o [illegible] anait fragad
in [illegible] bid sin uamair docl [illegible] oir

is uera liniad indise na liniad an bid [illegible]
[illegible] cuir [illegible]
⁊ [illegible] ⁊ [illegible] ⁊ [illegible] ⁊ [illegible]
[illegible] ⁊ [illegible]
⁊ [illegible] ⁊ [illegible]
an [illegible] ueniendo
[illegible] in [illegible]
[illegible] .i. [illegible]
[illegible] ⁊ [illegible]
[illegible] ⁊ [illegible] calud [illegible]
nabla [illegible]
[illegible] ⁊ [illegible]
[illegible]
[illegible] .i. [illegible] apeil [illegible]
[illegible] apeil [illegible] ⁊ in fogm
apeil sin philosophanus Ketum cle
mentis [illegible] caput et orientis
.i. feil clemintina [illegible] do [illegible] an
[illegible] ⁊ is do [illegible] luig [illegible]
cuirlis nahaimsira go [illegible] ⁊ [illegible]
sin donall [illegible] Ghrac dai
mis [illegible] nabla ⁊ [illegible]
uair and [illegible] ⁊ uair eile ni [illegible]
⁊ uair eile nis mo [illegible]
aimsir nocte ⁊ in fogmuir [illegible] and
[illegible] ⁊ uair eili fuair [illegible]
[illegible] ⁊ ingeimri ina [illegible]
mis no fuair golmuth Uillt eili
.i. olt apis gocom [illegible] nah
uig ⁊ a caibdel indoig bis deis cuir
li dambia ingailh glan giod dafag
aid [illegible] glan [illegible] go [illegible]
[illegible] ⁊ is amt is follaine [illegible]
[illegible] anuirgi Uillt eili

bit apir agut supubi nairiuncu
b. cuirmi inporuch. a tos nacoda
Joenet raterim do cablan Jodh
bch Joo raich Joosill l. doclitou
ib geala lora amanbliib Jarnarag
g Jacoimpuig lebainoi al mont quad
im gabimait antosi nahalmoint J
acaith in imlan inan bit l. acicino
dobiain dib Jacabaint dona dainib
dailig cuirt J donding bir amnac
ncoi Joolucc napaith Gacraimpa.
infinc cuib poraich dobrraich J do
bugloru Joorail cuac Joomencuy
al Jdospinancha Jdopaciencia J
dolactuca Jdo bair pinell Jpsillio
acosinubli J is mait macoll do cuy
and dambia ingaili puan anpis
nacaicin J. is maitt cuimin J
nacaid pong nap nain nairua
id F maitt pulaid Jrue cuimin J in
dig agambia gaili anpan Jgaoit ine
ls nacaich aren con iad gnaid poc
nuid eanbuich nairis Jdoinilagad
Jnabit enjaod danubstanc and
Cuitt. sil bit apir agut goirr
in coicis lit anbaindi dogaili puan
Jinoenan dongaili et J is incuib
doigin baine goirt andra tiamp
Antim. caith noim nabiadu
ib et J nacaid l. dair digi J nacai
a nasun baindi daich integrar
ne cumanta oir is doine pisiniat

Ol apir po suiub mon incoimgid
nanech oina mara taid na hoir pra sna
J nanech lcat oina mar a taid na h in
donit doac nos J is uime gnis lg n
lt dongl. gohinmeadonac cogaint
mait in bioh J a nos tad gomait J gu
himlan la bl gopogaimill J is uime
gnit nanoid inopong caich bias
gorotinoir n oir caitid nair and
neith incoidraca pul dobirit dani
suido U. cabroil doncoir J doscript
N oir J in complex is bicig n lenec
ib corpaili pollaminnig iat gidg
is uime dit aid nadaoine oganneich
plin J naneich ciniaid J naslnadi
onty lnoar J nani coin nanech pla
.i. naneich moca l. boga mas oligid
andike bit ac imuigi J olt a bias
an docuich in gomime l ol lira
roind dopollamnig nair naslnai
oinib oir tmuigh ansoinu ind mus c
icid neich peime dosi pulang teim
Lcaiuige goluac apuil somait
luct antraotair caitid neich pora
ig ch pinra oir is iat gni is uime caich
prisinrotair oir gseh nanech nos
cuig einaid nanech bbe am
pliggl. t rubstanc is gohinmu
on gioag bit cim gopogaimillac
J is daingne goluil iad J is uime
gni is olcra antat onch J t gin
isolcra anoil naneich beiribe

Column XXV

n aran bit fliuch ocus is maith iat Gideadh is olc aran na pastae *Et* is riaghail orlethon condlighear an biadh lenus do na méruibh intan taidhillter e do shecna oir s righin e. *Et* nimaith na neithi róstuighthi connaimhter tar oidchi ocus cumdach orra aid na neithi ro-meithi ar deiredh na coda In taibstinens measuidha is ro-árd in eighes e ocus is uime sin a dubairt g[alen] *Commedo ut uiuam non uiua ut commedam* . is cum beith am bethaigh caithim ocus ni cum caithime bim am betaigh Gidhedh deirur sa cét partegul d'*aforismorum Senes facilime ferunt ieunium* .i is ro-urusa lis na en-daoinibh in trégimus d'fhulang ocus is iad na sen-daoine on arrsuigecht sin ocus innsein na daoine óga ocus aindsein na macaoini ocus ainnsein na sen-daoine on sendacht. *Et* mar in cétna is leór ansacht le lucht lenna fiond treighinus d'fulang ocus re lucht fola deirgi go hinmedonach ocus ni féduit lucht lenna ruaidh na lenna luibh a fulang Gidhedh is ferr fuilngit lucht lenna duibh e na lucht lenna ruaigh ir is luigha in tes disgaoiles indtu ocus is mó caithaighius a ní ar an gnimuighend *Et* do cuir in fersaightheoir fersadha ar follamnughadh na slainti *Si uis incolumem si is te redere sanum curas tolle graues irasci crudere profanum* .i mad áil let beith fallain uir imsnimh trom dít ocus creit gurub dimaoin duit ferg do denamh

Column XXVI

Parce mero scenare caue nec sit tibi uanum pergere post epulas sompnum fuge meridianum i coigill fíon ocus sechain suiper ocus nai bu dímaoin let céimniughadh léis na coda ocus sechain codhladh in medoin-láe *Non teneas minctum nec cogas fortiter anum* i. na conaim ar th'fual ocus na hégingh go láidir do shuigi *Et* ataid ersadha eili ar in fín *Dat uinum purum tibi ter tria comoda primum* i. ataid naoi ocamhuil do beir in fíon glan duit *Uires multiplicat et uiscera plena relaxata* i mdaigh na brígha ocus lagaid na hinde línta *Confortat stomacum ceribrum cor dat ibi letum* i. nertaigh an gaili ocus in inchinn ocus do bir in croidhi subaltach ocus do ni lánacht ocus togairmigh an t'allus ocus geuraigi in t'indtlecht ocus do ni foirbhearteos lo na cáirdib Gidhedh bit misui maillí ris conach truaillter a oipriugh oir teid an limaoinus gach ní dibh so an égmais an misuir. *Et* o ibter an fíon uair and go leighinech bit an fersa so agut *Potus tarde datus multos facit cruciatus* i dobeir in leoch ibter go deiginech piana imda *Item*, gnathaighter camel go minic oir do bir an oél go deghbalaidh ocus foghnuidh an aghaidh in iemafhuai ocus comhedugh ar ruailledh na leanna anntu ocus is uime sin adeirui *Non moritur homo commedens sepe*

Column XXVII

de cinamomo .i inté caithius camel go minic ni recha d'ég do truailledh na lendann o1 toirmisgid e dambia an follamhnughadh go maith osoin amach. *Et* dlighear afis go dligheand an t'uisgi beith glan ocus glantur an t'aci go h'ealadhanach le teine maith muna faghtur glan gu nadurdha e *Et* is lór so ge do fédfuigh moran eili do rad ann

F-i-n-i-t.

Nott let guruba sea hinduibh dlighear an adharc do cur maille fuiliughaidh In cé inadh a clais cúil incinn ocus folmaighe si ona ballaibh ainmidhi ann sin ocus fóirid tinneas in cind gohairighi ocus eslainti na súl ocus glantur (ocus) salchur na haighchi ocu do ní inadh na cuislinni ren aburtar scfalica. In dara inadh .i itir in dá slinnen ocu folmaighe si ann sin ona ballaibh spirutalta ocus do ní comfhurtacht an disnía ocus a asma ocus an ortomia ocus do ní inadh na cuislinni renabur mediana In treas inad ar bunuibh in righthigh ocus folmaighe si ann sin ona lamhuibh ocus fóiridh in seregr bis inntu. In ceathramadh h'inadh itir na háirnibh ocus in leasrach ocus folmaighi ann sin ona ballaibh oilemneacha ocus do ní inadh na cuislinni renabur basilica I cuigedh h'inadh ar lár na sliastadh anagaidh lipra ocus brotha na sliasadh ocus brotha i cuirp gohuilidhi ocus ar galardha fuail mar ata stranguria ocus an agaidh gach ui eslainti dambia is na ballaibh ichturuca. In seiseadh inadh i ar lár na colpad ocu folmuighi ona

Column XXVIII.

cosaib and sin ocus do ní inadh na cuislinni renabur sofena ocus togairmidh in fu místa

℥ i unsa, ʒ i dragma, ℈ .i. sgruball

Peritisimus Omnium *rerum ipocras et cetera* i eochair gach uile eólais ip(ocras ocus ro-urail eólus ocus aithi báis ocus betha nan uile corp do[s]gríbhadh in beth degindaigh ocus acur a comhraigh leis fein ocus d'órdaigh a cur fona cinn san alucad areagla na fellsamh ele d'aghail dirradais a ruine ocus secired a chroidhi

Et a cinn móirain dh'aimsii nadiagh sin tainic in t'impir i sesar ocus ro-fhurail a uaigh ocus in t'allucadh d'oslucadh d'iaraigh indmuis i óir no leag no seod inbuadh *Et* as e ní dofiit and bogsa cumdaidh ocus do togbadh he ocus do hoslucead he ocus is ní fuair and cairt ina roibe dirradus ip[ocrais] ocus do fhurail an t'impire atabairt d liag(ac) a cuirp ocus a colla fein ocus amustosio a ainm an leagha do chídis na puba dó ocus do leag an cairt ocus ar na tuigsin do foillsid don impire gurab e dirradu ip[ocrais] do bi ann ocus tasgelta báis ocus bethid an cuirp daena *Et* do laba ip[ocras] aitús do comarib báis doleth an cind *Et* do raghi do bia tinnus sa chean ocus at a pull na sróna singalur sin bás sa ceathramh la dhég ar fhithit. *Item* a neach ar a bidh frenisis

[illegible]

dechmad mo .i. inter caithr caisel
gomminic nisfacbes do [illegible] na
[illegible] oir toirmisgid e dam
bia anfollamnugud go maith oroin
amach [illegible] ar is gon [illegible] tancad
tuirsi [illegible] glan 7 glan [illegible] anteir
gabhat [illegible] lectine maith munara
[illegible] glan gonadairidat [illegible] is lorr fo
[illegible] mo nan [illegible] dosaidan
[illegible]

Nocht le guba .c. hindiuli olcan
adaire do ciur maill friut .3. inad
aclais ciul incind 7 folmes onaball
ainmidi aisin 7 folsit tinteas incind go
[illegible] nisful 7 [illegible] is fale
nahaig [illegible] 7 doni inad na cuirsi fren
abuir [illegible] sefalica .4. inad .i. icin
darlitten 7 folmes aisin onaball
spiritalta 7 doni comstas anoirne
7 anasma 7 anoirtomia 7 doni inad
na cuirsi frenabuir mediana .3.
inad [illegible] bunnib indus [illegible] 7 folme
aisin onalaimib 7 foirit in [illegible]
[illegible] bic incind .8. hinad icnc
hairnib 7 il leasraic 7 folmigid aisin
onaball oilsimia 7 doni inad
na cuirsi frenabuir basilica .9.
hinad airlair na slastad anaghaidh
sron 7 brota na sliasad 7 [illegible]
golnus 7 [illegible] fuail mar acaise
[illegible] 7 anag [illegible]
bia is naball [illegible] tuca .10. inad
.i. airlair na colpa 7 folmaigid onc

corpaib anoirsin 7 doni inad na cuirsi
frenabuir sofena 7 tosgaired inn
[illegible] nirta
3 .i. tempa .3. i. [illegible] .3. i. [illegible]

Pertissimus omnium
[illegible] 7 cetrina .i.
eocair gach uile eolais [illegible]
eolus 7 [illegible] 7 [illegible] lecoir
[illegible]
[illegible]
fona cinn 7 analucad [illegible]
ele [illegible] 7 [illegible]
Racim [illegible]
tainic [illegible]
fuail [illegible]
[illegible]
[illegible]
[illegible]
[illegible]
[illegible]
[illegible]
[illegible] colla fer [illegible]
[illegible] anleaga [illegible]
[illegible] 7 deleag ancaint
7 [illegible]
[illegible]
7 tarsgelta [illegible]
[illegible]
[illegible]
[illegible]
apuill na sfiona [illegible]
[illegible] la [illegible]
[illegible] an neach gabis [illegible]

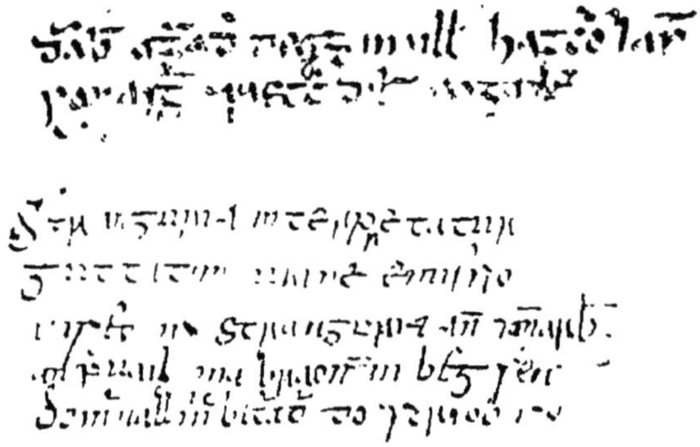

COLUMN XXIX

mbadh a gruadh dearg maille hataomlacht san aghaidh ocus re tere eaghtha sa ghaile

Stranguria interpretatur guttatim urine emissio i. sedh is stranguria n-iomarbadh an fhuail ma bhraonaibh mbeg sen Domhnall mu bethadh scriobh so

TRANSLATION

CHAPTER I

Col. I REGIMEN SANITATIS EST TRIPLEX, that is, there are three aspects of the Regulation of the Health *Conseruatiuum*, that is, guarding, (or maintaining the healthy state), and *Preseruatiuum*, that is, fore-seeing, and *Reductiuum*, that is, guiding backwards (restoration) as Galen shows in the third Particle of his Tegni. *Conseruatiuum* to the healthy men, it is right *Preseruatiuum* to those who are going into unhealth and to those of debility, it is a duty. And *Reductiuum* to such as are in illness, it is necessary. Nevertheless *Seruatiuum* is called *Preseruatiuum* sometimes as Hali says in the third Particle of his Tegni in the sixth Comment (and) ten and two twenties (the fifty-sixth Comment). And yet I say that it is from things similar that the conservation is made, as is said in the same place, *Si uis conseruare crasim quam accepisti similia similibus offeras*, that is, if you wish the Complexion which thou hast taken to thee to be retained give things similar And so, it is things similar altogether in degree and in form that should be given to the moderate (abstemious) body, and the body that declines by natural disposition (away) from moderation, things similar should be given to him according to form and not according to degree because of the desire (disposition) he has towards falling as Averrhoes says in the sixth book of Colleget And if you say that inaction is not taken to him from the similars

Col. II. as Avicenna says in the chapter upon the Signs (or indications) of the Complexion in the second Section of the first Book where he says that it is from *tota species* the members act upon the food, I say that it is from *tota species* of the member

(the stomach) that digestion is made and from the warmth (heat) as instrument as Averrhoes says in the fifth Book of Colleget regarding the stomach of the bird called Struccio, that more readily (quickly) is the time in which a big (piece of) iron is melted there from *tota species* than in the fire and so it is in this case Or I say that similars take no effect in the things that are without life yet they may do well in the things in which there is life Nevertheless the bodies which decline (depart) from moderation they should be regulated (nourished) by things similar according to form while they are in the moderation which is proper to them, and without being similar as regards degree, for the degree should be lower in the (case of the) food than in (that of) the body if given for its nourishment. And these people should be nourished with healing food, for it is with food that is (really) food the temperate Complexion should be nourished. *Uerbi gracia*, that is, Hali says in the third Particle of his Tegni commenting (upon) this text *Calidiora calidioribus, et cetera*, that it is necessary to cure the warm body or the body which departs from the equableness of its two degrees with things (that are) hot in the first degree. And these are called cold things, for the low heat is "cold" in the mouth of the physician, and it is therefore that some say wrongly, understanding (interpreting) that text, that it is with cold things the hot bodies ought to be conserved, and that is a lie Yet it may be prevented (fore-seen) or saved by things
III with lower degree than the body desired to be preserved Yet, nevertheless, the regulation (or treatment) which is called *Reductio* it is with cold things on the contrary (side) and in degree that it should be done (carried out) Still it should be understood that it is with things hot and low that the hot bodies should be preserved, and the cold bodies with cold (and) low things, and the dry bodies with things dry (and) low—*et cetera* And it is evident that those of black humors (of the Melancholic temperament) should be regulated with things cold, dry and low, and these are hot, moist things and not singly

but in compensation for the Complexion of black humor as says Commentator the Damascene in the second Particle (and) in the fifth Comment and three twenties (the sixty-fifth) that the wine is hot and dry yet he says that it is hot and moist in compensation for black humors and so also I say in this case And so also regarding the cold Complexion (that) it should be regulated with things cold, moist (and) low, and these are hot, dry (and) low things Yet if a Complexion of white humors (of phlegmatic temperament) has fallen by a hurtful fall towards coldness and moistness it should be regulated (treated) by hot, dry (and) high things—and that is the guiding towards the contrary. Further, these things ought to be studied in order to preserve the health, namely, Appetite (or disposition) and Quantity (of food) and Order and Time of year and the Time or Hour of eating and Age and Habit. And we have said concerning the appetite lately that it should be similar in degree and in form or in form only and not so in degree for as was said at first that low things are similars to the cold Complexion because low hot things are called cold by the physician and the cold is (a) similar to the cold thing, and also everything in which there is life it is hot [to be so classed] and it is therefore it should not be understood that the cold things are not similar(s) to the human body but that the cold low things are, and these are hot things in the mouth of the physician. COL. IV.

THE SECOND CHAPTER—OF THE QUANTITY OF THE FOOD.

The Quantity of the Food, that is, it should be eaten when it is desired, for Aristotle says in Epistula ad Alexandrum, *Dum adhuc apetitus durat manum retrahe,* that is withdraw thy hand towards thee and (while) the appetite is (yet) remaining with thee And Avicenna says in the chapter which speaks of the regulation of the things (to be) eaten and drunken (that is Concerning Food and Drink) *Ita comede quod sint reliquie*

desiderii, that is, you should so eat that you have a remnant of desire (for more) left, for it is better to multiply the times (to have meals more often) than a great quantity (at one time) And it is better to eat a little in two times than a great deal at one time because the food that is eaten at one time in large quantity it cannot be digested and it will pervert the power of digestion of the stomach then, and the error (perversion) that is made in the first digestion if (while) it is great is not corrected in the second digestion as Commentor Damascenus says in the first Particle in the sixteenth Comment. And it is therefore that it does not nourish dutifully then And it is for that reason that Avicenna says in the third Book that the greedy men will not grow And also the food that is taken in unreasonable quantity it will cause constriction and that is a cause of corruption through the absence of coolness, according to Hali in the third Particle of his Tegni And it is the sign that a person has eaten enough that there comes not from the eating of the meal any increase of the pulse or diminution in the breathing, for this will not happen but because the stomach closes (presses) upon the diaphragm, and it is therefore (because of that) the breath is small (and) frequent, and the need for coolness of the heart causes the pulse to increase, since there is no weakening of (upon) the strength Other signs are that there is no change upon the (appearance of) the urine nor upon the motions and upon the bowels particularly that hypocondria is
Col V not reached (caused) and without suffering cramps or flatulence or heaviness or weakness (faintness) and without sickness (desire to vomit) or *apititus caninus* (dog-appetite) nor falling (failing) of desire (for food) to be upon him nor laziness of mind, but that he can study after a meal as he did before it, but alone (indeed) while the food falls and the digestion begins, because the offensive (un-praisable) fumes then arise and they cause sleep and prevent study And further he should be without sleeplessness and he should not have the taste of the food when he eructates—for if these are as we have said it shows that the

food has been moderate in quantity. Yet the habit ought to be considered here, if it is not very bad, as may be seen. And I say also regarding the drink that it should not be in that quantity that the food is a-swim in the stomach as the case is with drunkards. And it is therefore (that) the thing which some say that it is well to get drunk once a month is a lie, as Averrhoes shows in the second Particle of the Canticles in the third Canticle (and) ten over twenty (the thirty-third) where he says *assensus ebrietatis simel in mense est erroneus*, that is, it is wrong to agree to the drunkenness one time in the month, for, though of the things which more benefit the natural heat (it is) the wine taken in moderation and of the things that do it harm (to the natural heat) and to the brain and to the senses (it is) it, when it is taken in excess, and it is therefore he says there that the water of honey is better for those who have weak nerves, than it (the wine). Yet nevertheless a little wine may give comfort to the old men as he says there (in that place) Yet Avicenna says in the chapter which speaks of the regulation of the water and the wine *Pueris dare uinum est addere ignem igni in lignis debilibus*, that is, it is (like) putting fire upon the head of fire on weakly wood to give wine to youths Nevertheless give it in moderation to the young men, and to the old men in the quantity he wishes, indeed they ought to have it in good quantity I say that the quantity he may desire should be Col VI given to the old man because of the agedness and that is the moderate old man who will desire as much (only) as he is able to digest and he is a very discreet man And yet the old man from his very-agedness (see Voc *Sen*) he should not be given that much, for such people are exhausted and foolish and small is their heat for they are like a lamp ready to drown (go out) as is said in the first Particle of the Aphorisms and it is therefore that Galen says in the same Particle commenting upon this canon *Potus indigenciam soluit et cetera* it is therefore I ask (I question) is it before the meal it should be given or (immediately) after, and it will be seen that not before the meal for

Avicenna says in the chapter which speaks of the regulation of the water and the wine *Sapiens debet sibi prohibere ne ieiunus uinum bibat*, that is, the wise man should spare himself from drinking wine upon first eating and it should not be given after the meal for Avicenna says in the same chapter *Uinum post quod libet omnium ciborum est malum*, that is, the wine is bad after every meal (or food), and he says in the chapter which regulates the thing eaten and drunken *Uinum post cibum est ex rebus magis impedientibus digestionem*, that is, of the things which more greatly prevent the digestion (is) the wine drunk after food, because it makes the food bore (pass out of the stomach) before it is digested. And the wine upon the meal is not proper, according to Avicenna in the chapter which speaks of the regulation of the things eaten and drunken where he says *Oportet ut post comestionem bibat quis et non in hora comedendi* it is necessary that it is after (the) eating a person should drink a drink and not in the time of eating And he says a little before that *Non est bibendum donec cibus de stomaco descendat*, that is, a drink should not be drunk until the food falls from the stomach. *In opossitum*, the common custom is against this, drinking the wine with the meal and after it. I say that it
VII is not right (to take) the wine before the meal in the time of health. Yet it is necessary sometimes in the time of illness, that is, when there is the greatest fear of the failure of the strength the wine will not hurt—as is evident in the syncope which comes from exhaustion (weakness of strength). And I say that in that time (in such a condition) it is right (to give it) before the meal and after it And when it is made as an argument (given as a reason) that it should not be given upon the meal I say, according to Avicenna in the chapter which speaks of the regulation of the water and the wine, that two *biala* drunk with the meal will not hurt the person who has made a custom of it, and so also to the healthy man after blood-letting. Nevertheless, the ordinary practice should be observed here if it is old or if it is not very bad, and it should be for-

saken (given up) at that time after each other (gradually) and not suddenly. And, this it is, that I understand through this word *briala* the measure (so much) as is taken in one drink only, that is, as much as a person can take without change of breath, that is, without straining the breath or stopping it unwillingly. I say also that the wine is bad after every food but after (until) the food is digested and has fallen, except in *caninus apititus* where tender things should be given first and then wine, and that is necessary treatment. Nevertheless, it is not right to take wine after food from which evil humors are generated or before or at tho time of eating, as Avicenna says in the same place, for it causes that evil humor to penetrate towards the exterior parts of the body and it is therefore that such people err as would desire to drink wine after evil (indigestible) foods (in order) to digest them, for it (the wine) goes before the digestion and it makes the body heavy.

It is therefore I say, briefly, that the wine may be given in small quantity after the meal and not in great quantity, and that it should be given to a person accustomed to it and to a person after blood-letting—and not to give it to any other person except in time of great thirst and in the other cases put (stated) in the chapter which speaks of the regulation of the water and the wine And when he says that the wine is not right with the food I say that it is thus the words of Avicenna should be COL. VI understood when he says that it is after the meal the drink should be drunk and not upon it, that is, that it is after the mouthful (bite) is swallowed and not while it is in the mouth that it should bo drunk, for to drink while food is eaten causes a glut—and that is what Avicenna calls quantity. The food is more effectual (more nourishing) by that a person should not drink upon the meal anything that puts the food in motion (forces it forwards) or anything that puts it too quickly in motion, otherwise it (the food) is separated from the stomach and it is put a-swim Nevertheless a little may bo drunk after the meal so that the food may be co-mixed and stirred about

well, and without making (any) very great fundament and without drinking to excess after it but (rather) to increase the number of times of eating, and without increasing the ordinary quantity And it is therefore I say that there are three (kinds of) drinks, that is, *Potus alteratiuus*, that is, the alterative drink, and *Potus permutatiuus* that is the co-mixed drink, and *Potus delutiuus* wash-away drink The alterative drink, it is before the food it should be taken—such as are the syrops and the heating drinks The co-mixed drink, it is upon the meal it should be used, a little being eaten and then a little drunk, so that the proper mixing is made The wash-away drink, furthermore, after the meal, upon the making of the digestion (after digestion), and after the falling of the food out of the stomach, it should be taken—or in the time the food is leaving it (the stomach) And it is therefore that Averihoes says in the second particle of the Canticles in the ninth Comment (and) twenty, as the water which is poured into a boiling vessel stops the boiling (so) the water or the drink that is put at the end of the food which is being digested in the stomach (it) will prevent the digestion and it is therefore that not much should be drunk after the meal until the digestion is completed in the stomach But it is effectual towards the digestion to bear thirst after of
IX the meal Nevertheless it is not possible to declare the quantity of the desirable (the give-able) things from proved writings as Galen says in the third Particle of his Megathegni, yet let it be done according to the judgment that is near the truth and let it be confirmed according to proofs (experience) and practice

THE THIRD CHAPTER—OF THE ORDER.

Of the Order of Diet or the Eating of Food This is it, that is, when a person rises in the morning let him stretch first his hands (arms) and his chest and let him put clean clothes on and let him then expel the superfluities of the first digestion and of the second digestion and (of) the third digestion by the

mucus and superfluities of the nose and of the chest for these are the superfluities of the third digestion and then let him rub the body if he has proper time because of the remnants of sweat and of dust which are on the skin, for the skin is porous and it will draw towards it everything that is near it according to Galen in the first Book of *Simplici Medicina* And then let him comb his head and wash his hands and his face out of cold water in the summer and out of hot water in the winter and let him wash his eyes with water (which has been) held in the mouth and warmed there, dipping his second finger in it, for that will drive away the veils of the eyes and it will cleanse them. And let him then rub his teeth with the leaf of the melon in the summer and with the skin of the yellow apple in the winter. And then let him say his Hail Mary or any other (similar) thing which he may desire After that let him make effort (exercise) and moderate walking in high (elevated) clean places and let his food be prepared so that he may take food the first time after that exercise what time desire begins naturally And let him not take it (the food) before it (the desire) and let him not delay (beyond the desire) for Avicenna says in the chapter which speaks of the things eaten and drunken that the endurance of hunger beyond Col. X
habit (over the usual time) causes the stomach to fill from corrupt humors and there comes then a heavy fullness of red humors, drawn towards the mouth of the stomach so that the food cannot be eaten by natural desire (healthy appetite) though he should wish it. And a person should not eat to satiety as we have said before and only one food should be eaten at the one table (that is at one time) for Avicenna says in the above-mentioned place *Nichil deterius quam cibaria multiplicare et in eis temporibus prolongare*, that is, there is nothing worse than to eat too many different foods (at one time) and to prolong the time of eating, and it is therefore that he says in the end of the chapter *De regimine cibi* that it is sufficient for the old men to eat flesh-meat alone in the morning and bread only at

their supper, and let them not take immoderate (or exceptional) foods at (any) one time. Nevertheless if several (kinds of) food be eaten at one meal it is better to give the mild things first and the fat things then (afterwards) or the contrary of that, for when the mild food is eaten after the fat food it is quickly digested and the fat food is not, and it will be in that time seeking a way out and it cannot get it because the fat food is below, and it comes of that that the one is mixed with the other and they are all corrupted. Yet if one understood (rightly) how to equate the food to the stomach so much of the fat food should be given at first in proportion as the lower part of the stomach is warmer than the upper part Yet it is not possible or not easy to do that and since you disregard what should be done incline towards the mildness (the tender things) as Avicenna says in the chapter (upon) The healing of Quartan (fever) in the second Particle of *Regimenta Acutorum*

L. XI Item, do not take raw food on the top of half-cooked food And it should be therefore understood that the food abides in the body before it is entirely digested sixteen hours as Averrhoes says in the second Particle of the Canticles and the same is said in the last chapter of the sixth Book of Colliget though nine hours are said in some books, and that is a lie, for it is possible that the scrivener found a certain number written and he did not know what it was and he made a mistake in the writing (copying) and it should be sixteen hours and the reason for that (is) because Avicenna says in the chapter *De regimine cibi* and Averrhoes in the Canticles that it is correct feeding to eat food three times in two days, that is, twice on (some) days and once (on) the other day And sixteen hours should be between every two times of these (that is, of taking food) so that the two natural days (in which there are eight hours and two twenties—48 hours) shall be divided level-ly (equally) into three portions And the reason for that is if a mistake was made in the day on which food was eaten twice that it may be corrected on the morrow by eating (only) once, and *e contrario* for every evil that is done by the filling (the excess of the one day) is cured by the emptiness (of the next) and *e contrario* as is said in the second Particle of the Aphorisms Yet Avicenna says in the third Book (and) in the thirteenth Section (and) in the third Tract which speaks of the delay of the descent of the food out of the stomach *Remanencia equalis cibi in stomacho et egressionis eius est illud quod est inter duodecim horas et uiginti duas*, that is the usual time between the remaining (from its arrival) of the food in the stomach and its leaving is between twelve hours and forty through the slowness of the working of the digestive powers. And it is therefore I say that from the time fatty food goes into the stomach that it remains there six (hours) or in the places of the other digestions, for the chyle is tenderer than the bread and therefore it is quickly changed into red blood and red blood is quickly changed to rose in the pores of the members And Avicenna comes with this remark (namely) the food digested in all the members COL. through sixteen hours so happening without being assimilated to them in that time. Still, from weakness of the stomach, and from the fatness and from the toughness of the food it will remain sometimes through (as long as) eighteen hours or through twenty hours as is shown in indigestion of the stomach, and when a person eats hurtful foods of some kind which remain sometimes in the pores of the stomach through a month or (even) through a quarter of a year as I have heard from truthful men that they vomited foods and medicine some times in the same quantity and substance as they were taken a month before then. Furthermore it needs be shown that milk and fish are not right on one table nor wine and milk for they predispose a person towards leprosy. And let not a very hot electuary be taken soon after food nor any one thing diuretic for they will pervert (corrupt) the food, burning it or putting it in motion too quickly. And it is therefore that the drageta made of Maratrum and of Anise and of the like is bad immediately after the meal. For it is better to rest standing or to make (take)

a gentle walk after the meal as Rufus says *Modicus incessus post prandium hoc est quod michi placet*, that is, it is agreeable to me an easy walk after the meal Nevertheless to make great exertion after eating (whether) by walking or riding will corrupt the food and will prevent the digestion. (But) after that (the meal) take a moderate sleep as was said in this Canon *Uentres hieme et uere* that it is well to understand the extent to which the sleep helps the digestion. Still, the sleep and the non-sleep that goes beyond moderation is wrong, as is said in the second Particle of the Aphorisms, and let it be done in the night for Hippocrates says in the first Particle of the Prognostics *Sompnus*
XIII. *naturalis est qui noctem non effugit et diem non impedit*, that is, the natural sleep which does not avoid the night and does not prevent the day Nevertheless many men make day of the night, sleeping in the day and awake in the night—and that is very bad Yet, you ought to know that it is on the right side you should at first sleep for it is so that digestion is better made because the livers are (then) under the stomach, and you should afterwards turn upon the left side so that the food is not drawn towards the livers before it is fully digested, and then (again) turn upon the right side so that the thing (part) which is digested in the stomach is more easily drawn towards the livers And this may be learned from Avicenna in the chapter which speaks of the thing eaten and drunken and in the chapter that speaks of the sleep and of the sleeplessness And he says there also that to begin by lying on the belly will give great help towards the digestion because the natural heat is retained and because it is surrounded and it is therefore it is increased Still, a vain (shallow) sleep is bad and to sleep quickly after food is bad for the sight. And sleep of (in) the day is bad if it is not made in nearly a sitting position and that is good after the meal and in the summer but yet in that time, only a little. And it is therefore the versifier says *Aut breuis aut nullus sit sompnus meridianus*, that is, let the sleep of the middle (of) day be brief otherwise don't let it be

done. Nevertheless if it is done before the meal let it be done of a morning till sunrise according to Hippocrates in the second Particle of the Prognostics. And it should not be done and (with) the mouth open for fear that bad air may go in and prevent the digestion. And let the head be well raised in the sleep and let him be well covered with clothes—according to Avicenna—and that is very good for (towards) the digestion ITEM, The diseases of the mind are here considered, and it is concerning this that the versifier says *Sit tibi mens leta labor et moderata dieta*, that is, have a cheerful mind and moderate diet and take exercise And greatly does bathing in sweet water Col. X suffice but that there is no food in the stomach. And let the supper be short or light unless the habit is against that, for regarding the digestion that is made during sleep it were better that not more (or not a greater quantity) were eaten at night Yet as the sleep is made so very soon, before the food falls from the mouth of the stomach, it is therefore that too much food at night so greatly hurts the sight and it is therefore that there are many verses upon this matter (on this cause) *Nocturna cena fit stomaco maxima pena*, that is, the supper of night is great pain to the stomach *Si vis esse leuis sit tibi cena breuis*—if you wish to be light let your supper be short. And there are two other verses upon the same thing *Scena breuis uel cena leuis raro molesta*, that is, it is rarely that the short or light supper is injurious. *Magna nocet medicina docet, res est manifesta*, that is, the healing art teaches and it is a clear thing (manifest) that the large supper hurts yet more *Sume cibum modice modica natura fouetur*, that is, Eat (but) a little food, for nature is satisfied with (from) a little. *Sic corpus refice ne mens ieiuna grauetur*—it is so the body is known to be satisfied that the mind is not heavy (not dull) because of the abstinence (from food) [when it remains clear without food] and yet take the food from thee (leave it off) when the nature sooner demands it

ITEM, let the urine and the faeces be voided (expelled),

and let them not for any one reason be retained beyond the time in which it is the habit to evacuate them, because they make constriction in the sides (parts) and singing in the ears from flatulence rising upwards (antiperistalsis), or a stone (in the bladder) or hydropsy from the holding of the urine. That is for thee John from Hugh O'Cendainn.

L. XV. *Nec minctum retinere uelis nec cogere uentrem*, that is, do not desire to hold thy urine nor to force thy middle (*uentrem*), that is, beyond the time in which it is right, and it is therefore that it is not well to be on the stool too long and (not well) to make forced squeezing And it is therefore that the urine should be given (passed) six times in the day with the night for that is the (whole) natural day—and the evacuation (of the bowel) twice or thrice in the same time as these verses say. *In die minctura fit sexies naturali tempore bis tali uel ter sit egestio pura*

THIS IS THE FOURTH CHAPTER—OF THE TIME.

Regarding the time, that is, the time of the year ought to be observed for something of heed should be given to the age and the country and the time as is said in the first Particle of the Aphorisms. And yet let fat food be given in full quantity in the winter because it is said in the same place *Uentres hieme et uere calidissimi sunt natura*, that is, the internal cavities are very hot by nature in the winter and in the spring, and the sleep will be very long It is therefore that plenty food should be given and the times of eating should not be frequent for the heat is not short as in the summer but long (great) according to the extension through abundance of the spirits Nevertheless the heat will be small in the summer taking warmth for the warm body more [*maior extensiue extensione raritatis sed non extensione quantitatis*] And the food should incline towards hotness in that time, and it is apparent from that what is well said regarding the heat of the young men and youth (generally).

In the spring however the food should be moderate but

inclining towards a smaller quantity because of the fullness that was done in the previous winter.

Yet, in the summer the food should be mild going into COL. (inclining towards) coldness and that is (means) mild in quantity, that is, (only) a little should be given at one time for the substance (the sum) of the (bodily) heat will be small in that time being spent and dissipated because of the external heat And if food mild in its substance is given it will be burned from the fiery heat And it is therefore that Galen says in the Canon *Uentres hieme et cetera* that the heat will go external in the summer to co-rejoice with the similars and it is therefore it is weakened (diminished) internally.

In the autumn, again, give the food in small quantity and it should be inclined towards warmth and moistness, and there are verses upon this *Quantam uis sume de mensa tempore brume* eat the quantity you wish of food in the season of winter, *Tempore sed ueris cibo moderate frueris* but use food moderately in the season of spring, *Et calor estatis dapibus nocet inmoderatis* in summer evil is made (comes) of the immoderate foods. *Autumpni fructus extremos dant tibi luctus* the fruits of autumn will give thee sore weeping.

THE FIFTH CHAPTER—REGARDING THE TIMES OF EATING.

The time of eating (the proper time) is when there is true hunger as we have said in the third chapter above And it is better in the summer (to choose) the time that is cooler, that is, before sunrise and at the time of vespers—in the evening. And the time of need (when it is really necessary) is the time in which food should be taken, and it is therefore that Galen says *in libro De regimine sanitatis* that no person should be compelled to observe the Rule of Health but the person who is not prevented (from following it) from any other compulsory cause and who has his desire (choice) free in every one thing (a man COL.

who is thoroughly well). Yet, in the winter, let the time that is warmer be chosen and so also of the spring and of the autumn, for those (warmer times) are apportioned towards the summer and towards the winter, for it is in the portions that are nearer to the summer of them that the time should be like the time of summer and the portions which are nearer the winter let the time of moderate warmth be chosen.

THE SIXTH CHAPTER—OF THE HABIT, OR CUSTOM.

The habit of diet should be maintained unless it is very bad (unless it disagrees or is injurious) and if it is so it ought to be departed from slowly (not too quickly) and therefore the habit which conforms with natural things should be maintained. And if it should depart (only) a little from them it should still be continued. Nevertheless if the departure (from nature) is great it should be directed back and (yet) not suddenly, as we have said And yet let those of bad regulation (habit) take heed to themselves for though it does not show on their countenance (even if the effect is not immediately apparent) it will yet show (later on) very effectively—they shall feel it—as Avicenna says. And therefore, those who say that they can fill themselves often with food and that no hurt comes to them let them take heed to themselves for they shall be hurt, for if God took revenge upon every one sin the first time after it was committed (that is immediately) there would not be a (single) man in life, and as is all Nature, that is, God, it is so that Nature is ordered in man, that revenge (restitution) is not made the first time (or immediately) but after a season. *Item*, there are some people who eat more of fruits than of other foods, and they do so wrongly, for
XVIII. every fruit makes a watery blood unprofitable (innutritious) and it is corrupted Nevertheless astringent fruits should be eaten after food if the middle (intestines) is relaxed—as are pears and coctanas and apples But the roasted apples before a meal will relax those of red humors (of choleric temperament), and the

raw apples are more astringent and every kind of them is greatly so, for the sweet apples are less astringent, and the sour apples are more so. Yet the bullaces and the raisins and the figs it is before the meal they should be taken as Isaac says *in Dietis particularibus*. Nevertheless the common custom is against this badly for this causes constriction from the milder things and it is therefore that they should be eaten with ginger for this fights against every corruption which comes of the fruits—according to Avicenna But it is better to avoid fruits altogether And it is therefore that Galen tells in the book upon the Regulation of Health that his own father was a hundred years in his life (lived a hundred years) because he did not eat fruits. *Item*, there are some people who prefer the tails of beasts rather than the other parts, and other people (prefer) the heads and other people the bones—and so of the other parts It is therefore that this verse says *Pisces et mulieres sunt in Caudis meliores uel dulciores* it is in their tails that the fishes and the wives are better or sweeter, but that only means that the fish is less cold in its tail than in the other parts of it because of its movement (or activity) Nevertheless it is easier to digest the other parts as is manifest COL. X regarding the belly of salmon and its like Nevertheless, that part which is in greater motion is the part that has less superfluity (that is less gross) and it is therefore the better part of the animals which men eat, if all other things are equal. Therefore let the more tender part be chosen which has some motion and is of better taste, for the part that tastes best nourishes best—if other things are equal And yet the verse says *Non ualet in iecore quod dulce est in ore*, that is, that thing is not good in the livers which is sweet in the mouth And it is of simple (single) sweetness that is to be understood.

Nevertheless I say of the nuts here, that there is not among all the fruits, after the figs and the raisins, a (any) fruit that is better than them, and it is therefore the verse says *Dic auellanas epati semper fore sanas*, that is, say that the nuts are always healthy for the livers.

Furthermore I say, namely, that such as would desire to indulge in co-reaching should not do so with the middle (stomach) full but after the finishing of the first digestion and the second digestion and half of the third digestion, and (I say) that it should not be indulged in (made) often, for that greatly weakens the stomach and the whole body, and it hurts the sight very greatly for it puts the eyes into great depth (it causes them to sink greatly) clearly.

XX. Of the Blood-letting, indeed, it should be understood that it should not be over-practised, for Avicenna says in the chapter Of Blood-letting that the too frequent blood-letting causes apoplexy, and Galen says in the ninth chapter of his Megathegni *Minucio ceteris euacuacionibus uirtuti maiorem debilitatem infert* the regulation (or practice) of blood-letting more greatly weakens the vitality of (than) all other practices, and the reason for that is that red blood is more akin to the nature (of man) than all other humors (fluids) It is therefore that its practice in the time it is excessive most greatly weakens, unless the man is young and has a complexion of red blood (has a ruddy complexion) and he is resting and using of flesh meat and of other foods which nourish well for that condition demands that blood should be let more seldom (less often) for fear of Quinsy and internal ulcers—than would be the case in another person (of different temperament). And the rule which Damascenus gives in his own Aphorisms in the second Particle (and) in the nine and fortieth Comment should be observed, that is, if a person in his youth practised to let blood four times a year it should only be let thrice (in the year) at the end of the fortieth year and once only at the end of sixty years, and after ten and three score or four score years it should not be let at all Notwithstanding, it is the mediana (vein) that should be let at the end of sixty years and the basilica at the end of forty years for it is not right to

XXI. let the cephalic (vein) beyond the end of forty years at the outside, for that will blind a person and it will pervert the memory.

The chosen time of the year, indeed, for the blood-letting, that is, the spring and the autumn. But the blood-letting of the spring is the better, for there is not one thing which preserves a person against the diseases of summer as the blood-letting of the spring does, according to Avicenna Yet it is in two portions the time of the whole year is divided according to the people, that is, the summer and the winter. And the blood-letting should not be in a very cold time nor in a very hot (time). And it is therefore that those err who would wish to let blood about the feast of Stephen and about the feast of John Baptist through (because of) the coldness of the one time and through the heat of the other time. But it should some times be let about Christmas to save from the illnesses which come of the filling (the excess) accustomed to be done commonly in that season.

Concerning the side on which it should be let, indeed, the versifier says *Estas uer dextras, autumpnus iempusque sinistras,* that is, the right hands in the spring and in the summer, and the left hands in the autumn and in the winter. And he says also as regards the Moon thus, *Luna uetus ueteres iuuenes noua luna requirit,* that is it should be let for (in the case of) old men when the moon is old and to the young men when it is new

Regarding the diet after blood-letting. It should be understood that great error is then (often) made, for there are men who would like to drink and to eat a great deal in that time to make the blood again which they have lost, and it is therefore that (only) a little should be drunken and eaten Yet more of wine should be drunk in place of (to make up for) the less food then, or as they were accustomed to, because it is easier to satisfy with drink than it is with food. COL. Yet, avoid cheese in that time and fat flesh and salt fish and fruits and anger and exertion and be not close to a fire and do not make co-reaching and do not make but a small supper and it is therefore this verse is good *Prima dies uene moderacio sit tibi sene,* namely, let thy supper be moderate the first day of (after) the blood-letting Nevertheless the other verses are lieing which would put (one) to activity and to exertion

And if you wish to know what time begins the (proper) seasons of the year they are found in these verses *Uer petre detur estas et iurule sequetur quam dabis urbano autumpnus simphoreano*, that is, the spring in (at) at the feast of Peter and the summer at the feast of Urban and the autumn at the feast of Simphorean *Festum clementis ieniis caput est orientis*, that is, the feast of Clement is the head of the beginning of winter. And this is according to the astrologers who always put the seasons to even-ness (who divide the seasons rigidly) and not so the physicians but they call the moderate time of the year spring, and it lasts sometimes during a month, but one time it is less and another time more The summer, indeed, it is a very hot season, and the autumn it is sometimes hot and another time cold according to different weather, and the winter is a very cold season altogether. Furthermore, namely, it should be understood that the eggs and their custard benefit such as are after blood-letting if the stomach is clean Nevertheless, if they are got in an unclean vessel they are very easily fouled, and they are the more healthy if broken into water Furthermore,
COL XXIII you should know that the right time to eat this pottage is at the commencement of the meal, and it is made, in the winter, of "kale" and of mallow and of sage and of parsley or of the white heads of leeks boiled and strained and mixed with milk of almonds And I say that the almonds are an excellent fruit eaten whole, as they are, or with the skin taken off them, and given to the men who have had blood let and to those who are wasting and to those of phthisis. In the summer, indeed, a pottage of borage and of bugloss and of violet and of mercurial and of spinache and of patience and of lettuce and of the tops of fennel and parsley with the like—is proper, and it is well to put avens into it if the stomach is cold. The pea, however, should not be eaten except with cumin. and let not beans or peas be eaten new or old except with salt and cumin, and those

who have a weak stomach and flatulence let them not eat them for any reason. Nevertheless the soup of peas is good (sufficient) and it relaxes, but let there not be anything of the substance (the solid part) of the pea be (left in the soup) Furthermore, understand that the milk greatly hurts the cold stomach and (but) it does not (hurt) the hot stomach, and for that the right thing is sour milk in the summer The butter, indeed, let it be eaten before the foods, and let it not be eaten after a drink, and let not the top of milk (cream) be eaten after the supper, or curds and whey for they are constringent and tough. It should be known Col. also that great injury is caused by the raw things such as the oysters, and the things half raw as are the birds that are badly roasted, and it is therefore that good cooking of the food and well roasting and completely (throughout) is little less than half the (work) of the internal digestion—or, to boil it well externally, and it is therefore that those err who eat too hurriedly (or greedily) for they sometimes eat hurtful things before they are brought to their attention (before they notice it)

THE SEVENTH CHAPTER—OF THE AGE AND TEMPERAMENT.

The Age and the Complexion—it is almost entirely by things similar that they are regulated (nourished) Nevertheless, the young men will digest more of fat things and of hard things than the old men because of their agedness and the sons (or youth generally) the moist things, that is, the tender or soft things, for the diet should be renewing (restorative) and (only) a little should be eaten (but that) frequently And those given to study should be nourished like old people, for the studying dries them, so let them eat tender things according to their sufferance (as they can bear them) so that their blood is replenished quickly and well. Those who labour, however, let them eat roasted fat things for these are the things that resist (the waste) of labour For though the roasted things are moister

within than the things cooked upon water from the moistness of the substance inside, yet they are dry outside and they are altogether more solid, and it is therefore that they are difficult to separate from their heat and therefore they are the more
XXV. difficult to digest The things that are cooked in bread they are moist and (but) they are good. Nevertheless the pastil bread is bad. And it is a very broad (comprehensive) rule that the food which adheres to the fingers when it is being touched should be avoided, for it is tough And the roast things kept over night are not good (even) with a covering upon them, nor the very tender things at the end of the meal. The moderate abstinence is a very high treatment, and it is therefore that Galen said *Commedo ut uiuam non uiua ut commedam*, that is, it is to be in life that I eat and not for eating that I am in life Yet, it is said in the first Particle of the Aphorisms *Senes facilime ferunt ieiunium*, that is, the old men more easily bear emptiness, and these are the old men from their agedness, and then the young men, and then the youths, and then the old men from their age. And so also those of cold humors fully enjoy to suffer emptiness (hunger) and those of middling red blood (well-blooded people) but those of red humors or of black humors cannot suffer it. And yet those of black humors bear it better than those of red humors for the heat is less which they set free within them, and they spend more upon the thing (or work) upon which they employ themselves (they have less resistance). And the versifier has put (made) verses upon the regulation of health *Si uis incolumem si uis te reddere sanum curas tolle graues irasci credere profanum*, that is, if you desire to be whole put heavy sorrow from thee and believe that it is vain (foolish) of thee to make
XXVI. anger. *Parce mero scenare caue nec sit tibi uanum pergere post epulas sompnum fuge meridianum*, that is, spare wine and avoid supper, and do not think it foolish to have a walk after the meal, and avoid the sleep of the middle-day *Non teneas minctum nec cogas fortiter anum*, that is, do not retain thy urine and do not constrain too strongly thy seat. And there are other verses

upon the wine *Dat uinum purum tibi ter tria comoda primum*, that is, there are nine (thrice three) cases (or comforts) which the clean wine gives thee *Uires multiplicat et uiscera plena relaxata* that is it multiplies (increases) the strength and it relaxes the full intestines. *Confortat stomacum cerebrum cor dat tibi letum*, that is, it strengthens the stomach and the brain, and it will give thee the light heart, and it will make (give) boldness (courage), and it will call forth the perspiration, and it will sharpen the intellect, and it will give assistance to the friends (it will promote friendship) Yet let moderation be along with it so that its working (efficacy) may not be perverted, for all these (good effects) will be undone without the moderation. And because the wine is sometimes drunk finally, remember this verse *Potus tarde datus multos facit cruciatus*, that is, the drink that is drunk finally will give thee many pains. *Item*, let cinnamon be used frequently for it will bring the mouth to sweetness and it will suffice against the cold rheum, and it will prevent the corruption of the humors in them, and it is therefore it is said *Non moriet homo commedens sepe de cinamomo*, that COL. X
is, the person who eats cinnamon frequently will not go to his death from corruption of the humors for that is prevented if the nourishment (regulation) is well in other respects from that outwards. And it should be understood that the water must be clean, and the air is cleaned scientifically (quickly) by means of a good fire, if it is not found naturally clean. And this is sufficient though a great deal more might be said here

IT ENDS

Make a note that it is in six positions the horn should be put in bleeding (cupping) The first position—in the furrow at the back of the head, and it will empty (draw from) the animal parts there, and it will relieve headache especially, and diseases of the eyes, and the filth of the night (upon the eyes) shall be cleansed, and it will serve or deplete the region of the vein called

Cephalic. The second position, namely, between the two shoulder-blades, and it will there draw from the spiritual parts, and it will comfort dyspnoea and the asthma and the ortomia and it does (controls) the area of the vein called Mediana. The third position, namely, on the roots of the forearm and it will draw from the hands and it will relieve the seregra that is in them The fourth position between the kidneys and the buttock, and it will there draw from the organs of nutrition (the nutritive parts) and it influences the province of the vein called Basilic The fifth position—on the flat of the hip, against the lipra and eruption of the hip and eruption of the whole body, and against urine disease, such as stranguria, and against every disease in
Col. XXVIII. the parts leading thereto. The sixth position, namely, upon the flat of the calf, and that will draw from the feet, and it does the area of the vein called Saphenous, and it will call forth the monthly blood.

℥ that is Ounce, ʒ that is Dragma, ℈ that is Scruple.

Peritisimus omnium rerum Hippocrates *et cetera*, that is, the key of all knowledge (is) Hippocrates, and he commanded that the knowledge and the prognostics of the death and the life of all [human] bodies should be written (at the end of his life) and that this should be placed along with himself in the coffin, and he ordered that it should be put under his head in the burial, for fear the other philosophers might get his "Arcanum" and the secret of his heart

At the end of much time after that, the Emperor came, that is, Caesar, and he ordered the tomb to be opened—seeking treasure, that is, gold or gems or precious jewels And the thing he found there was a shapen box which being lifted and opened what was found in it was a document on which was the "Arcanum" of Hippocrates And the Emperor ordered it to be given to the physician of his own body and flesh and Amustosio was the name of the physician. He saw the people, and he read the document, and having understood it he pointed out to the Emperor that it was the "Arcanum" of Hippocrates and the prognostics of death and of life to the human body. And Hippocrates spoke first of all regarding the signs of death pertaining to the Head, and he said if there is pain in the head and swelling of the nostrils that signifies death upon the fourteen and twentieth day (34th). Item, the person on whom there is Frenzy, if his cheek is red (flushed) with his face puffed with COL defect of digestion in the stomach.

Stranguria is (to be) interpreted (as) the emission of the urine in drops (and) that is not a trifling (small) matter. *Donald MacBeath* wrote this.

The first post-script beginning in Col. 27 would seem to be a personal MacBeath note based upon practical experience and observation—for I have not been able to trace its origin otherwise. It would seem also to be in the same handwriting as the text, so far.

The second post-script introduced by *Peritissimus omnium rerum Ipocras* is in a new hand without doubt, and most probably that of one of the MacBeaths themselves. At the middle of the fourteenth line down, another and coarser hand takes the same incompleted matter up. This is almost certainly that of James MacBeath, whom we find making other additions to the manuscript in the year 1598—and long after the O'Cendains and the O'Kearneys had finished their work—when the book as it stands was in the family possession. From this we must learn that the *Capsula Eburnea*, presently to be referred to, was also, and continuously, in the hands of the MacBeaths

In a collection of classic, medical, Latin tracts called *Articella*, which was, I think, first published at Venice about the middle of the fifteenth century, the piece *Capsula Eburnea* appears along with tracts from the works of Phylaretus, others of Hippocrates, Johannus Damascenus, Galen, Celsus, Avicenna (the Cantics), and others. It is headed *Liber Hyppocratis dictus Capsula Eburnea qui in ejus sepulchro inuentus fertur.* My edition was printed in London in the year 1519.

The Tract is introduced as follows—"**Peruenit ad nos quod cum Hyppocrates morti appropinquaret percepit ut uirtutes iste scripte ponerentur in capsa eburnea et poneretur capsa cum eo in sepulchro suo ne aliquis eam detegeret. Cum ergo uoluit Cesar uidere sepulchrum Hyppo. peruenit ad ipsum: aspexit ipsum: erat aut valde percepit ipsum renouari et fabricari et corpus ejus si integrum inueniret deferri sibi quidquam foderet sepulchrum inuenta est in eo hec capsa eburnea: et in ea iste uirtutes: delata est ergo Cesari: qui in ea aspiciens: Misdos amico suo fideli tradit**"—from which, when compared with the Gaelic rendering, it may be seen that the parallel is not very even between the two

It would seem that the MacBeaths attached some importance to this tract, and it is surely very interesting, if its history is true, even if it is of no meaning to us in this time There was a desire to continue it, but James was certainly not the man to do it. It has, however, been done. It was used as base for a Chapter in another Gaelic MS which lies at the Museum (Egerton, 159), and as it must be of interest for purposes of comparison, I give here a part of it which more than covers the post-script

Tionnsgainter dirydus ypo. ann so *Peritisimus omnium rerum ypocras et cetera* **i. eochair gach uile eoluis ypr rofurail**

eolus ocus aithne bais ocus betha nan uile cp̄ dosgriobadh ina bhetha deighionaigh ocus do furail a cur inn camruigh da h'adhlacadh leis ocus a cur fona cenn aregla na fell*samh* ele d'fag*bail* a dirraduis ocus a rúin ocus s*e*rci a c*hroidh* ocus intan tainig in t-empire i Sesair augustus a gcionn treimsi f*a*da do f*u*rail in uadh d'oslug*a*d d'iarraigh innmus ocus óir ocus leg loghm*or* ocus ocus t'séd mbuadha ocus is e ní fuair ann bogsa comduigh ocus do h'osluig*edh* e ocus do f*uair*n ann cairt ina raibhi dirradus yp. ocus do furail in t-empir a tabhairt do liaigh [a] cuirp ocus a colladh fein .i. amustotio ainm in legha ocus do creidi dais [daéis] na popuil idir a raibh dhó ocus do leighi an cairt ocus arna tuigsin dó do foillsich don impir gurb e diorradus yp do bi ann ocus tailsgelta [the first *l* has *punctum delens*] **báis ocus betha an cuirp d*ar*e*nd*a ocus do labair artús d[o] c*omartha* bais d'leth an cinn ocus adubairt dambia tinnis isin cend ocus at isin adhaigh ocus cosachtach minic ocus a lamh clé ar a ucht g'minic ocus a lamh do cur com poll a tsrona gominic si[ngalaidh] in bás isin 4 la dh*ég* ar fichid. Tuilleadh .i i nech arambiadh frenisis dambia a gruadha derg maille h'atcomall san aigaid ocus re droch dileaghtha sa g*aili* si[ngalaidh] bás an x. la. Tuilleadh mata an eslaintisi maille h'allus ocus a cluas ocus a fiacla dobeith fuar ocus na cuilfedhe [? cuislinne] go rengam*ail* ocus saotur dobeith arna corruibh brugad maille esbuidh eisdecht si[ngalaidh] bás isin .x. la. etc.**

The tract is translated in full (Eg 159), but it does not follow the Latin very closely, especially in the matter of "critical days" The forms of the language are distinctly nearer to those of our own time, and the writing is in many respects like that of Adv. III Both are almost certainly of the late sixteenth or the early seventeenth century

Since I finished my work on this text, I have examined MS Adv. LX, and I find that my note, p 3,—1511, must be corrected. The MS was written at Dunolly, Argyll, in the end of the sixteenth century and the beginning of the seventeenth—and the signatures, which are frequent, leave no room to doubt that Maconochie or *Duncan's Son* cannot be equated with the Connacher who wrote this book The signatures are always **i ɔqbair, i conqbhair,** and **y ɔqbair**—and this is one of the oldest and most famous names in the whole tradition and history of Ireland, easily contemporary with the Christian era It is Connor now, but Connacher is much nearer to the original The adherence to the Irish generic **i** and **y** for Irish **ui** and modern **O'** is very interesting and suggestive, and one wonders whether these men of Con-acht may not after all be the Kun-etae of Herodotus

NOTES.

Column 1

LINE

1 I here give the whole of the First Chapter from the Latin text of 1501 for purposes of comparison with the Gaelic

Regimen Sanitatis est triplex, Conseruatiuum, Preseruatiuum et Reductiuum ut innuit Hali tertia particula tegni can 19 Conseruatiuum competit sanis, Preseruatiuum neutris, Reductiuum egris Sed Preseruatiuum nominatur Conseruatiuum ut dicit Haly tertia particula tegni (τέχνης) commento 55 Dico ergo quod Conseruatio fit per similia—unde tertia particula tegni Si vis conservare crasim qualem concepisti similia similibus offeras Corpori ergo temporato debent dari omnia similia in gradu et forma Sed corpori lapso lapsu naturali debent dari similia in forma sed non in gradu propter inclinationem quam habent ad lapsum ut dicit Auicen. 6° Colliget ultra medium lib cap de regimine complexionum malarum Si dicas similia non patiuntur a similibus sibi dicit Auicen libro p[ri]mo, fen 2ᵃ capitu de signis complexionis Dico quod membra agunt a tota specie in cibum et ideo dico quod digestio fit a toto specie membri per calidum tanquam per instrumentum sicut dicit Auer. 5° Colliget de stomacho structionis quod in minori tempore dissolvitur ferrum quam in igne a toto specie Sic dico in proposito vel dico quod a similia non fit passio in rebus inanimatis sed in rebus animatis bene potest fieri Corpora ergo lapsa regantur cum similibus in forma quando ipsa sunt in temperamento eis debito sed non in gradu quia gradus debet esse remissior in cibo quam in corpore nutriendo Et debit talis regi per cibum medicinalem quia per cibum absolute complexio temperata absolute regi debet dicit Haly tertia particula tegni in commento illius Calidiora calidioribus indigent adjutoriis quod lapsum corpus vel calidum ab equalitate per duos gradus debet regi cum calidis in primo gradu vocat frigidum, quia calidum remisse frigidum est in ore medici. Et ideo aliqui errando dicunt ex Haly quod calida debent conservari cum frigidis, hoc est falsum Tamen preservari possunt cum frigidis remissis et in gradu remissioribus quam sit corpus preservandum. Sed reductio debet esse perfecte in opposito latere in eodem gradu Hic tamen sciendum quod calida debent regi per remisse calida et frigida per remisse frigida et sicca per remisse sicca, etcetera Sicut melancolica cum remisse frigidis et siccis remisse et hoc est cum calidis et humidis non absolute sed respectu complexionis melancolice Sicut Commentator Dama. particula quinta asso commento 67 quod vinum est calidum et siccum tamen respectu melancolie est calidum et humidum. Sic dico in proposito quod ita complexio flegmatica debet regi per frigida remisse et humida et hoc est per calida et sicca remisse. Si tamen complexio flegmatica sit lapsa lapsu accidentali ad frigitatem et humiditatem tunc debet regi per calida et sicca intensa et hoc est reducere Consideranda tamen sunt in regimine sanitatis, qualitas, quantitas, ordo, tempus anni, hora prandendi, consuetudo, et etas De qualitate cibi iam dictum est quia debet esse similis vel in gradu et forma vel in forma licet non in gradu quia ut dixi prius remisse calidum vocatur frigidum a medico et simile est frigidum frigido Et cum hoc vinum omne calidum et ideo non est intelligendum quod frigida sint similia corpori humano nisi frigida in remisso gradu, quae sunt calida in ore medici.

6. Galen (Claudius) was born at Pergamos, Asia Minor, A.D 130. His father, a noted architect and mathematician, gave him a good education, intending to follow the study of medicine We learn from his writings that he studied under the best physicians of Smyrna, Corinth and Alexandria, and that he travelled widely in quest of knowledge. In his twenty-eighth year he settled in his native town, where he remained for five years He then went to Rome, where his skill soon brought him into prominence Envious of his great success as physician and teacher the other physicians made his position so uncomfortable that he went back to Asia, after a while again settling in Pergamos In A D 169 he was again back in Rome upon the invitation of Marcus Aurelius After some years in Rome, practising, lecturing, and writing, he seems to have returned to Pergamos, but little more is known of his life Neither the time nor the place of his death is known He wrote a great number of treatises upon medicine and philosophy—perhaps hundreds—but very many were lost at Rome, where his house was burnt He also

LINE wrote fifteen commentaries on the works of Hippocrates (See Col 6.)

7. **Hali sa treas partegul do thegni** *II in the third Particle of his* τέχνη. This most probably refers to the translation of Hali's works by "Constantine the African" under the title of *Pantegni*. Hali's most important work was "El Malika" or the *Royal Book*. He was a strong hygienist and an independent observer and thinker, basing his practice and his writings upon his determination of cause and actual experience rather than upon his teaching or learning. He died A.D. 994.

Constantine (1018-1087) was for a time teacher at Salernum and afterwards became a monk of Monte Casino

20 **tabhair neithi cosmuile** *similia similibus offeras* This doctrine is extremely comprehensive and valuable. It underlies to a most remarkable extent the great part of what is sensible and truly scientific in modern medical treatment. It simply means "See what Nature is doing and help it on." The homœopaths have made these words their chief corner stone, but there is no evidence anywhere in their literature that they ever understood the words in their original and philosophical sense In fact their practice, which they think is based upon this old teaching, is at once conclusive proof that they have not only not understood it but have perverted it into very strange ways. To a thoughtful student of Medicine, and especially of the surgical side, it is of abiding interest to observe how very much of all that is rational and assured in our treatment of the present time is referable to this venerable principle.

28 **Aueroys,** usually now written, Averrhoes—a corruption of his Arabic name, Ibn Roshd, or as we should say, Mac-Roshd. He was born at Cordova in Spain in the early half of the twelfth century, where his father was chief magistrate His early education was directed towards theology and philosophy He succeeded his father in the magistracy, and was also appointed Cadi of the province of Mauretania by the king of Morocco His learning and his great gifts were envied He was charged with having rejected the established religion, and, after being deprived of his offices, he was banished to Spain. Here again he was envied and persecuted, so he fled to Fez and after further persecution there, he was ultimately restored to his dignities by the enlightened Caliph Al Mansur. After an active life he died in Morocco in the beginning of the thirteenth century Aristotle was to him

LINE the greatest of philosophers He wrote translations of, and commentaries upon, the philosophy of Aristotle to such an extent that he was nick-named *the Interpreter.*

He wrote a compendium of medicine, called *Colliget* in translations, but a corruption of Arabic "Kullyat" meaning *Universal* The Colliget is frequently referred to in our Text

31. **Auicina**, now commonly Avicenna for Ibn-Sina, Arabian physician and philosopher, was born near Bokhara A D 980 Aristotle was his favourite philosopher He tells us that he read the *Metaphysics* forty times before he understood it He was very precocious, finishing his early education at the age of eighteen, when he began to practise as a physician Losing his father, at the age of twenty-two, he spent several years in travel, studying his profession, and then he settled down at Hamadan as private physician to a noble lady He was soon afterwards appointed Vizier to the Emir. On the death of his patron, the son and successor did not continue him as Vizier so he went into retirement, meanwhile writing diligently upon his favourite studies in philosophy and medicine. He offered his services to the Sultan of Ispahan and so came under the suspicion of the Emir, who put him in prison He escaped, however, to Ispahan, where he was received with great honour He lived and worked here in peace for fourteen years He died A D 1037 His principal medical work was the *Canon Medicinae*, often referred to in our text He also left many commentaries upon the works of Aristotle.

COLUMN 2

3 **Tota species** I have not been able to find out where this expression had origin It clearly means the same as our word *digestion* in its widest sense It seems to imply a big truth, namely, that digestion is not a matter limited to the stomach alone, but is a function of the whole body and of every part of it Our nails and our hair digest, select, and assimilate the elements of food that are proper to them as surely and as correctly as do our muscles and our bones The whole body is a digestive organ

"And from the heat as instrument" This also is a complete expression of actuality. The less heat the weaker function The higher heat the more life No heat, no life at all

LINE The words "form," "degree," and "high" and "low," "hot" and "cold," in this connection have no meaning, and can have no meaning in our day. They were artificial and *unnatural* concepts, of the empirical form of thought, which imagined man to stand apart from, and outside Nature The whole truth is well stated in the Sixth Chapter, "As all Nature is, that is God, and so Nature is ordered in man" Man is Nature, Nature's highest product and expression Man is the microcosm, Nature is the macrocosm In Heine's wonderful statement, "The Ego equals the non-Ego," the whole of wisdom is complete

20 **biadh is biadh** "cibum absolute"

24 **Calidiora calidioribus**, etc—the full quotation needs **indigent adjumentis**

25. **Cuttromacht** is here used in its original and best sense of *equipoise*, or, as Latin has it, *equalitate*. In the modern speech it always means *weight* or *heaviness*

Column 3.

9 **Complex lenna duibh—lenna find—lenna ruaidh** These are the Complexions, Temperaments or Idiosyncrasies of the individual body—in older times called Melancholic, Phlegmatic and Sanguineous In the translation I have rendered the words literally. There is something of a general truth underlying these concepts, and the practice based upon them is not disregarded even in the present time *Crasim* is the Latin in Col 1 for **complex** from Gr *κρᾶσις a combination* whence *ἰδιο-σύν-κρᾶσις idiosyncrasy*, or as it occurs in Old English, "His bodies crasis is angelicall" (1616)

11 **an aithfheghadh complex lenna duibh** *respectu complexionis melancolice.*

12 **Commentator an Damasenus**—the Damascene Commentator, was "Janus Damascenus" Jahjah ebn Massiweih, a famous physician and teacher of Harun, and a prolific translator from the Greek He lived 780-857

28 **don cháil gustrasda** nearly misled me into making it *gustatory*, but it is really for **gusan dtrath so** *lately* or *up to this time—de qualitate cibi jam dictum est*

COLUMN 4.

LINE

3. **Do chaindigecht in bidh**—Of the Quantity of the Food—*Quantitas cibi*, is the Heading of the Second Chapter of the Tract, although it ends the First as may be seen **Dlighear a chaithimh intan tochluighter e**, *it* (food) *should be eaten in the time that is desired* This is, of course, a simple commonsense observation, yet, not always acted upon. The word **caithimh** has a wide range of usage. **Gu meal 's gu'n caith thu e** *may you enjoy it and wear it out* is a kindly Gaelic wish when a friend gets a new suit of clothes **Chaith e a mhaoin** *he spent or wasted his means* **Caitheamh** is the disease *consumption* In our Text it is used of the *using, eating*, or *consuming* of food, always A little thought will show that the essential idea is the same throughout **Tochluighter** is from **tochluighim**, which I cannot find in the dictionaries, but throughout the text it plainly means *desire, disposition*, and *appetite* most frequently.

4 **Arustotul**—*in epistula ad Alexandrum* Aristotle was born at Stagira in South Macedonia, B C 384 His father, Nichomachus, was a physician of the race of the Asclepiadae who traced their descent from Aesculapius The profession of medicine was hereditary in the family of the Asclepiads, and Aristotle was seventeenth in descent from the founder of the family and the profession Diogenes Laertius tells us that Aristotle was with Plato at Athens for some twenty years, after which he went to take charge of the education of Alexander the Great for several years After this he had a school at Athens from 335 to 322 B C. when he retired to Chalcis where he died shortly afterwards Some of Aristotle's works are well-known. He was the founder of the Peripatetic School of Philosophy and the originator of the scientific method of investigation and of reasoning It is safe to say that no human being ever used language so precisely, so closely, and so keen-edged, as Aristotle used it for the expression of the highest efforts of the human intellect The best minds of mankind have strived to follow him He remains the supreme model of thought and expression and, as would seem, for all time

25 **do ní duinte ocus is cúis sin don mhorgadh** *cibus excedens debitum oppilat et est causa putredinis.* **Duinte** is from **dúin**

LINE *close* up, it is Lat. *oppilatio* which is explained in another part of the *Rosa* as "Oppilatio hepatis est constrictio seu coarctio seu clausio venarum quae sunt in hepate seu in poris et foraminibus quae sunt in substantia ejus" See Col. 14, 34.

26. **tre esbhuigh an indfhuartha** *propter privationem excitationis*—
34 **égintus innfhuartha in croidhi** *necessitas excitandi cordis*

28. For **innach** read **in[tan]nach**

Column 5

3 **apititus caininus** I have translated this literally as *dog-ish appetite.* It is a diseased excess of appetite usually now called Bulimia **Tuitim tochluighi** "*pigritiam*," *sluggishness*

7 This would read better and perhaps be more correct as **eirghitt na detaighi inmolta** The Latin is *vapores boni ascendunt*, and my statement in the Vocabulary should be so corrected—although the MS reading and the context are quite enough to have led me away

20 The sign 2 is used for **dá** *two* and with *a* superscript for **dara** *second* (23, 34) and for *est*, and for the terminal syllables **-da** and **-dha** Inverted ɔ is for **con** always as in **ɔtrardha**, **ɔgmail**, etc The old Latin ȝ for *ejus* is very neatly used in lȝ = **leighius** *healing* or *cure* Col. 7, 24.

25 **feithi anmfhanda.** The word **feith** is now almost always used for a *vein* **Cuisle** is the word in the Text for a *vein* (see Col 27), but in the later usage the word means more correctly an *artery*. This differentiation is desirable and even necessary The primary meaning of **cuisle** is a *pipe* or hollow tube The Latin is *nervos debiles*, but we have no word in Gaelic for *nerve* so far as I know.

27. **intán tosgaighius go himurcrach** *quando excedit debitum*

40 The spelling **imchubhaidh** shows that my rendering **imchubidh** might be better so spelled, but as I had it so set in type I have left it as it was The same is the case with the word **dlighear** which I have put in the Scottish Gaelic form throughout. In the division of words I have also leaned towards the Scottish forms rather than towards the Irish method of "eclipsis"—but this does no violence to the language

Column 6.

LINE

4 **duine ro-dheisgribhidech** *homo summe discretionis*

5. **an senduine on tsenordhacht,** lit *the old man from* (because of) *the old-agedness,* but the latter word seems to have a specific meaning apart from its etymology. O'Reilly renders it as "the fifth stage of human life, from 54 to 84 years of age" It is, however, very difficult to deny a kinship between it and the Sc Gaelic **seanair** *a grandfather,* which is usually taken to mean **sean-athair** or *old-father* It is, however, equated with *sen-ator* The *senex* of Latin was a man over sixty. The meaning of the Text is however quite clear It means a man old beyond the generally accepted old man In the second line we find **dona tshenduine on thsendacht** *to the old man because of his agedness,* but here in the sixth line, as quoted, *the old man because of his over-agedness*—the treatment is different The Latin in the younger case is *seni a senectute,* and in the older *seni a senio.*

6. **dibenta** *decrepiti.*

8. **lóchrand ullamh cum baithi** (leg **báidhti**) *lucerna parata extinctioni.*

9 **sa .c partegul d'amforismorum** This clearly refers to the Aphorisms of Hippocrates, for Galen makes the Comment It is, in my copy, the 21st Aphorism of the Second Book Λίμον θώρηξις λύει.

12 **Fiarfuighim** *I ask.* Compare **ag iarraidh** *seeking,* Col. 10. These words are part of the same verb but the one has initial **f** and the other has not. This **f** initial is not "organic", it does not belong to the first part of the original compound word **iar + fach** which is the preposition **iar** *after* It is called "prosthetic" It seems to be a matter of dialect and is very unstable See **osluigthi** (13) where Sc Gaelic would have **fosgailte** *open* It comes and it goes readily. It comes very often where it does not belong, and it goes, perhaps as often, where it does, *e g* the Preposition **ri** which was originally **frith,** Lat. **vert,** *turn* We have **feagal** for **eagal** *fear* in several districts, and other similar instances might be given

Column 7

5 **isin tshingcoipis** from *συγκόπτειν to cut short,* usually applied to fatal fainting coming from heart-failure

LINE

10. **dá (2) bhriala**—see the explanation seven lines down *as much as a person can take without drawing breath and yet not restraining it.* I cannot trace the word satisfactorily. *Bria* was old Latin for a wine-vessel, but it is not easy to see a connection with this *Bala* is *a mouthful* in Arabic and this may have been a miswriting It is certainly interesting that our own word even now for a mouthful is **bala-gum** In a text of 1595 it is *duas phialas*, but in the margin it has "*duas brialas est in autore*"

12 **déis cuislindi** lit *after the vein*, but used here and frequently in the Text for *blood-letting*—see Col 27

13. **Dlighear an gnathughadh do coimedh annso mad arrsaigh e muna fa ro-olc e** *the* (usual) *habit should be observed here if it is* (an) *old* (custom). **Arrsaigh** is not now in use and it does not seem to be etymologically related to **aois** *age*, for which it is frequently used in the Text **Fa**, again, is used here not as the prep **fa = fo** *under*, or as in **fadhó, fathrí** *twice, thrice*, but as the verb *to be* **fa = bha**. Compare Col. 17, 12

18. **claochlogh anala** *change of breath*—or between one breathing and another. This in Sc. Gaelic is **caochladh** with base **clóim** *muto, I change.* It is very finely used in the common speech for the great change of death. The idea of extinction is entirely absent—excluded. It is never used of the death of animals **Caochladh aghaidh nan speur** is *the change in the face of the skies* **Caochladh na h'aimsire** is the change or *transition* of the seasons The concept of essential continuity is as clearly implied in the word as is that of simple change **Chaochail e** *he has changed*—Eng he is dead

27 **san inadh .c. na** *in the same place* This single **c** is used as here in **cétna** *the same* It is also used for **cét** *first* in **c inadh** *the first position* 27, and for **cét** *a hundred* **goraibhi a athair fén .c bliadhan ina bhethaig** *that his own father was a hundred years in his life*—that is, of age 10.

Column 8

2 **taréis na coda** *after the meal*, is for **tar** *trans* + **éis** a *trace* or *footstep* It is always translatable as *after* even when combined with another prepositive as **déis** for **do + éis** It may take a personal pronoun as **tar a éis** *after it*, **dom éis** *after me*

14 **fundamínt** is the Lat *fundamentum*, but what the exact physiological intention here is I cannot well say. It may mean

LINE that the food was supposed partly mixed or dissolved and partly not, and that the latter was the *fundament.*

16 **contınoıdech** which I translated as *constringent* in my Essay, basing it upon Lat. *contineo* in the sense of *holding together, e.g.* **leighes contınoidech** *astringent medicine* will hardly do here The Latin is *multiplicat vices non quantitatem continuam, the unbroken* or *ordinary quantity.* O'Reilly gives **cointoımiodeach** as *customary*—from an old source

18 **trí deocha** *three kinds of drink*—Alteratiuus, Permixtinus, Delatiuus. The Alterative was supposed to effect a beneficial change in the body without materially affecting the fluids—the humors. The Permixtinus was a "mixed drink," but whether it had any fixed formula or any definite aim would seem to be impossible to know. The drink Delatiuus is rendered in Gaelic **ımairctech,** which means *removing* or *changing,* and the fact that it should be taken after the meal suggests that this was something like the purpose of it. The word is made up of **imm + aır + ıc** *to come.*

The "Appetiser," the "bottle of wine," and the "Liqueur" of civilisation are doubtless descendants of these three drinks, performing similar supposed service.

COLUMN 9.

1. **caındighect na nithead ıs ıntabhurta** *quantitas offerendorum* The prefix **ın-, ıon-,** signifies *fitness* or *appropriateness,* so **intabhurta** means *giveable* or what is right to give.

7. **D'Ord in Dıeta no Caıthme in Bhídh**—*Of the Order of the Diet or the Eating of Food.* This begins the Third Chapter as stated at the end of the previous paragraph

13. **coımleadh an corp,** *let him rub the body,* from **co + melım** *I rub* or *grind,* Lat *molo.* The same word is used for the teeth (24)—**coımleadh a fhiacla le duılle uircill . . . ocus le croıcinn an ubhaill buidhe** *fricet cum foliis citrulli et cum cortici citri*

23. **tursgar na súl** very likely a metathesis from **trus** *gather,* therefore, what gathers upon the eyes during the night—*illud enim aufert lippitudinem oculorum eosque clarificat* *Lippio* was an old expression for having sore or bleary eyes

32. **na gabhadh roimhe ocus na cuıreadh a faill** *non ante nec tardius*

Column 10.

LINE

2. **do lenduibh morguighthi** *with corrupt humors, pravis humoribus.*

3 **linadh tadhbais o l[ind] r[uadh]** *a heavy filling from red humors, venit repletio fantastica propter choleram contractam ad os stomachi.*

5. **lisin thochlughadh ainmhidhe** *with the animal* (natural) *desire, appetitu naturali.*

10 **prolongare**—it should be noticed that the loop on the stem of **p** is in front *before, pro* the stem, whereas in *per* it is after the stem—if the vowel is not superscript as in Col 1, 8.

16. **Ni gabdhaois biadha examhla an éinfheacht** *nec diversa edulia accepisse simul.* **Examhla** = **eu** + **con** + **samail** the negative of **cosmail** **Ein** *one* + **feacht** *time*—the word is not now in use, but it remains, if rather hidden, in the words **feasda** *for ever* and **fathast** *yet,* which are our present forms for old **i-fecht-sa** and **fo-fecht-sa.**

26. **meadughadh** here has a slightly exceptional meaning Usually the direct meaning is to *enlarge,* to *make large,* but here it means to *equate* the food to the powers of the stomach—to make the food "as large as" the stomach can use. The Latin has it well as *apportionare.*

30 **o nach feduruis cad is indenta** *quum ignoras quid sit faciendum*

Column 11.

13. **Proindiughadh orduighthi** *orderly* (or proper) *feeding*—to take food three times in two days **Proind,** the base here, is evidently the Lat. *prandium* "a dinner," but used in the general sense of a meal. Compare "post prandium" with **déis in proindighthi,** Col 12, 22

14 **Fathrí sa dá lá i fadhó ládib ocus einfecht lá eile** *twice in the* two days, *that is, twice on days and once* (only) *on the other day.* The modern language has lost these very useful forms **fadhó, fathrí,** etc. They should be restored.

This dietary may seem peculiar—one day two meals and the other day one, or three meals in forty-eight hours. A personal note may be excused. While on a long sea voyage two years ago, I found that the regulation three or four meals a day made

LINE me quite useless, and strangely enough I fell into this very way of two meals one day, and only one on the alternate days. The result was to me altogether excellent, and indeed surprising, and I have followed it more or less closely ever since. I can truly say that when I may depart from it I am in no way benefited, but distinctly the reverse This was before I knew anything of this Text or of its teaching.

25 **tuirlingha an bhiadh** in MS. Should be **an bhidh**

28 **uiginti duas** This seems to be an error. In the Latin texts it is always *sedecim*.

30. **tre moille oiprighthi na brighi dileaghthaighi** *propter tarditatem operationis digestivae*

32. Read **na[in] inaduibh** etc, *quam in aliis digestis*—a recognition that they knew digestion took place in other parts as well as in the stomach.

35. **is luath indtaighter** etc, *et ideo cito convertitur in rosem* (*in rorem*, 1595) *in poris membrorum*

COLUMN 12.

9 **gur sgeigheadur** *commoveant*

13. **Lubra**—the word seems essentially to mean, or rather to have meant, *leprosy*, when that disease was common in this country, but later the word seems to have come to mean simply "disease" in one of its coarser external forms Specific leprosy seems to have followed the Crusaders into Western Europe Lazar-houses were numerous in England from eleventh century onwards for more than five hundred years There was a leper-house at Canterbury in the eleventh century, and one was established in Edinburgh as late as 1591, and it was the end of the eighteenth century before the disease disappeared—in the Shetlands

14 **Lictuairi** a *lectuary*, an old form for electuary. Chaucer has it "Too late cometh the lectuarye"

17. **Drageta** This seems by some way of kinship to be the same as Fr *dragée*, a sweetmeat or comfit A form *dragé* is used in modern pharmacy for sweetmeat covered medicines

Rufhus—of Ephesus, a man very greatly in advance of his time (about 50 A.D) especially as anatomist

25. **Marchuideacht** *riding, horsemanship*, from old Gaelic **marc** *a horse*—W Cor. Br **march**

LINE

32. **tar modh amach** is rather unfamiliar It means that the sleep and the sleeplessness *which goes beyond manner* or is excessive either way, is bad.

COLUMN 13.

7. **Arson nan ae do beith faoi in ghaili** *because the livers are under the stomach* It is remarkable that the liver is always referred to in the plural form This implies that they knew the evolution of the human liver, and that morphologically it is a compound organ, or that they made no post-mortem examination or dissection of the human body, and that they derived their knowledge from observations upon the lower animals It is well known that dissection of the human body was even a rare thing in the old Schools from which our MS had origin, but in the Latin texts the word is always in the singular, in Gaelic only is it in the plural form

8. **diligher impog ar in taobh clé** *you should change to the left side.* The writing of **dilighur** which is wrong for **dlighear** shows that the writer was copying and that not intelligently The same sort of error occurs frequently In Col. 14, 10 **móran in bidh** was written **móran in biadh** but it was corrected and even then left wrong

22. **angar do beith asuighi** *nisi quasi sedendo.*

29. **o mhaidin go teirt** *mane usque ad tertiam*—to the "third hour"—after sunrise. O'R has **Teirt** *sunrise*

33 **cluthur le hédach gomaith e** *pannis bene contegatur patiens*

35 **measruighter aicidigi na h'anma** *acculentur animae reperientur*

COLUMN 14.

2 Note the contractions for **acht, nach** lines 2-3 The former is very often met with as terminal **-acht** and **-echt**, and the latter for **nech** *a person*

8 **sul toitis an biadh** *before the food falls*—**toitis** mis-written for **tuitis.**

16 **édrum** *light*, compare **édrom** line 4.

17 **ar an cétna** *upon the same thing* Note the contraction for **cétna**

19 **athumulta.** I cannot find this word anywhere It means

LINE "molesta," and is perhaps **ath-thum-alta** or as we should say *repeating* of the food

21. *res est manefesta*—a new way of writing *est.*

22 **teaguisgaigh an ealadha leighis** *the art of medicine teaches* This means rather that from the means used an instructive inference can be drawn If the remedy used, and directed towards a definite purpose, succeeds, then the inference is good that the diagnosis was right

32. **na fastaighter ar én cor iad** *nec retencatur ultra quam natura stimulat, let them not for any reason be restrained* or withheld. The verb is spelled **fostogh** in Col 7. The meaning here is that neither the natural inclination of the bladder or of the bowel should be for any reason restrained beyond the time in which it is the habit to empty them This advice holds true in our day—and with emphasis—when our most valuable lives are too often wrecked or lost from Appendicitis, of which this unnatural restraint of the bowel is almost if not altogether the simple and sole cause. It is not the farmer or the field-worker or the shepherd who suffers from Appendicitis, but the dweller in the office and especially in the drawing-room Without anti-peristalsis there would be no Appendicitis, but the very simple physiology of the matter cannot be entered upon here The advice is powerfully pertinent, and the explanation in the Text is quite complete—"**on gaothmuirecht ag impogh suas**" There is no need for any theory of Appendicitis beyond this A well-known English epitaph gives sound and sincere advice on this matter, but a friend has, for some reason, thought it would be better Latinised, and in *his* Latin

"Quacunque sis, efflate bis,
Retente, me—hic jacit!"

That retention of the urine may cause stone is not at all unlikely, but that it may and does cause syncope there can be no doubt.

34. **oir do gendaois duinte** *quia generant oppilationes*—see Col. 4, 25.

38. The last line is an interesting note, it is the signature of Hugh O'Cendainn, the writer

Column 15.

LINE

1. **nech** in MS. has the aspirate, wrongly.

8. **sa ló conoidchi** *in the day with a night*, oir is e sin in lá **nadurda** *for that is the natural day*—24 hours This preposition **con** is lost to modern Sc Gaelic although it remains hidden in a few old expressions **Slat gu (con) leth** *is a yard and* (with) *a half.*

16 **do leith na haoisi**, etc, *aetati, regioni et tempori.*

21 **na cabain inmhedhonach** *the internal cavitas, ventres*—the stomach and intestines.

25. **oi ni bfuil** *for there is not* **Oi** here is for **oir** It occurs so, and so often, in the Text that it becomes a suggestion the writer was tongue-tied or lisped It occurs Col 17, 4 and 26, where it is followed 28 by **oir** for **uair**

29. **doréir shínte in edluis**, etc It is very difficult to understand the concept underlying these phrases The Latin (which I have been compelled to put in the Translation) is just as difficult to understand The wording is not difficult but the meaning is

33 Note **q** with **m** superscript for **chum**, and in 36

35. Observe the reversion of the writing here to the previous line 34 and continued in the following 36. This is the rule in these MSS. and almost certainly for economy of space—see Cols 6, 32, 20, 6 **Mesurrdha** here is *temperatus*

Column 16

5. **da tucaoi** should be **da tuctaoi**

16. **tempore brune** = *tempore brumae* *Brūma* is more correctly the shortest day or time of the year—the winter Solstice or Christmas time It is really *brevissima* (*dies*) contracted It is here meant for the Winter or the cold time as a whole

20. Note the terminal contraction 2 for **-da** in **mesurrda** This, with and without the aspirating over-dot, is frequent Compare **mi-mesurrdha** 24

22. **in moderatis**—*immoderatis* **mí-mesurrdha**

33 **roimh an teirt**, etc., *ante tertiam et hora vesperarum.*

34. **uair an éigentuis** *tempus necessitatis*

LINE

37 **nach eidir le nech**, etc., *nullus potest observare tempus cibi sumendi nisi is qui non est occupatus in aliqua operatione necessaria aut qui liberam habet conditionem in omnibus.*

COLUMN 17

10 **Don gnathughadh** *Consuetudo Dietandi*

29 **ocus mar ata in nadur uilidh**, etc , *et sicut est de natura universali quae est deus ita de particulari in homine quia non statim punit sed in processu temporis*

32 **an c oi = an cét uair** *the first time* See Col. 15, 25.

36 **oir do ní gach uile thoradh**, etc., *omnes fructus faciunt sanguinem aquosum et inutilem et putrefactibilem*

COLUMN 18.

5. **lagaid na húbla rosdaighthi roim an qid[chuid] lucht l[enn]a r[uaidh]** *the roasted apples* (taken) *before the meal relax those of red humors—colerici*

7 **istipeda = is stipeda**, and so also at 9, *they are the more binding*

13. **Ysaac** (Ben Soleiman, 830-940) was a pupil of "Johannes Damascenus"—Col 3, 12. He made a special study of Foods, determining the value not only of the different kinds of flesh, but also of the different parts of the same animal Though a Jew (hence called Isaac Judaeus) he was strongly in favour of pork as a nourishing food.

27 **drong ele a gcinn ocus drong ele a gcnamha** This is perhaps the best example of Irish "eclipsis" in the Text It occurs with other initial consonants, as may be seen, but not at all regularly It is not unlikely that the Scottish tendency, which has quite done away with "eclipsis," was asserting itself at the time There is a superfluous **a** at the end of 27

29. **pisces et mulieres.** It is *uvores* in the texts available to me, and so it is rendered in the Gaelic—**na heisg ocus na mná**

COLUMN 19

1 **mur is folluis do tharr in bradain** **Mur** if not quite wrong would be better as **mar** **Mur** is the Negative Conjunction *if*

LINE *not*, but **mar**, which is here certainly intended, is the Adverbial *as*.

I was very nearly misled by **do tharr**, which I took for **do thár** *regarding* or *concerning*—the salmon. This, however, is the old **tarr** *the belly* of the salmon which is, as evidently was, considered the best and most digestible part. **Donnachadh Bán** finely sings of the "**Bradan tarra-gheal**" *the white-bellied salmon*. The Latin is *ut patet de ventre salmonis*.

2 **in cuid is mo bis ar gluasacht**, etc., *illa pars quae magis est in motu pauciores habet superfluitates*

8 **gluasacht hégin** *some movement*—a certain amount. Note the contraction for **h'eígin**—it frequently occurs.

9 "That which tastes best nourishes best"—a very neat expression and perhaps true all the way, yet the "verse" is against it.

14 **is don milsi oenda tuighter sin** *it is of the single sweetness that is to be understood. Single* here means the sweetness of one simple article of food as against the *compound* sweetness of made "dishes," or **neithi cumuisgtech**—see Col. 8, 20.

16. This contraction for **etir** is not common.

22 **an drong lerbáil coimriachtachain do gnathughadh** *qui volunt uti coitu.*

26. **gna a denumh gominic** should be **gan a denumh** *without doing it often*—simply bad copying.

Column 20

1 **Don cuislind umorro** begins the paragraph upon Blood-letting.

2 **aū** here is for Avicenna and not Averrhoes.

4 **Aphoplexia**. This word is a remnant of the old "evil spirits" concepts of disease. It is even now in English called 'a stroke." The idea was that the evil spirit came up stealthily and maliciously from behind and *struck* the unfortunate victim with a mortal, even if invisible hammer, so knocking him down, perhaps never again to rise.

> "Whilst Apoplexy, cramm'd intemperance knocks
> Down to the ground as butcher felleth ox."
>
> Thoms. *Castle of Indolence*

The same concept is in the word Epilepsy in which the malicious spirit was thought to jump or *leap* upon the victim

LINE unawares and held him under, writhing and foaming, during the fierce struggle. The Greek origins of these words are plain and their meanings also

5. **Meghathegni** = $\mu\acute{\epsilon}\gamma\alpha + \tau\acute{\epsilon}\chi\nu\eta$ the Great Work—see Col. 1, 7, note.

6. Note the reversion of the Latin quotation

9. **don uile fholmugad** (O'G.)

10. **gurob cara don nádur fuil derg** *that red blood is more akin to nature*—to the tissues of the body—than any of the other fluids This of course is quite correct. "Quia sanguis est amicus naturae plus quam alius humor."

12 **intan is imarcach e** *quando excedit*

13. **coimplex fola deirge** *a ruddy complexion* showing that he is full-blooded.

17. **squinancia ocus nescoidedh inmedonach** *quinsy and internal ulcers* The word **nescoid** is now limited specifically to the boil and *carbuncle—apostematum interiorum* is the Latin—but in the old time before the advent of our pathology its application was very wide and very indefinite

The genesis of the word is given in Cormac's Glossary as follows· Goibniu, the smith of the Tuath dé Danann, was at his forge making weapons for the battle of Moytura when something affecting the character of his wife came to his ears, and this upset him. "There was a pole in his hand, when he heard the story, Ness was the name of the pole, and he sings spells over the pole, and to every man who came to him he gave a blow of this pole Then if the man escaped a lump of gory liquid and matter was raised upon him, and the man was burned like fire, for the form of the pole called Ness was on the lump, and therefore it was named **Nescoid**, from that name **Ness** then, that is *a swelling*, and **scoit** *liquid*"—all which may or perhaps may not be quite true. **Ma's breug uam is breug chugam**

20 In both my Latin texts of 1501 and 1595 this is "secunda particula Aphorismorum commento sexto" without the **dá fithett** of the Text.

24 Read **fathrí acind [a] dara**

Column 21

3 **Uair toghnidhi na bliadhna** *the time of year to be chosen*—for Blood-letting—begins a paragraph The origin of the word

LINE **bliadhna** the *year* has not as yet been very conclusively explained. It is **bliadain** in old Irish, and O'Reilly (*Introduction*) argues at some length that it is the Keltic **Bel-ain** the great *circle of the god Bel* or the Sun—for **aine**, G **fáine**, Lat **annus**, and **anus** was and is *a ring* or *circle*, and see Dr. Macbain *in voc* **Bealltuin** and **Bliadhna**

5 **oir ni fuil én ní coimedus nech ar eslaintibh in t'samhruigh mar do ní cuisli an erruigh** *for nothing protects a person from the ills of Summer* (so well) *as does the Spring blood-letting* **Coimedus**, which I translate *protects* here, is the same word as often occurs in the sense of *seeing* or *foreseeing*—see Col 1 The Preposition **ar** is here used very clearly in the sense *against*.

14. **um feil Stefain ocus**, etc, *about the feast of St Stephen and about the feast of John Baptist* The Preposition **um** is here nearer to its original form than is usually met with In modern Gaelic it is inverted to **mu**, although it still remains in the compound Prepositions as **umam**, **umad**, **uime** and **uimpe**, etc Its cognates are W. **am**, Cor. and Bret **am** and **em**, Gaulish **ambi**, Lat **ambi**, Gk. **ἀμφί**.

19 **Don taobh as an dlighear a ligen**—*Concerning the side on which it should be let*—a paragraph

23. **do leith an ré** *regarding the moon* **Ré** is here used in its classic sense for *the moon*, which is now **a ghealach** or the *white one*. This should be a paragraph

27. **Don diet d'áithli na cuislindi**—*Of the diet after the Blood-letting*—another paragraph

31. **macht cadfarligettur i** This is one of the places in which I find a difficulty in rendering the contraction which reads **macht** as **maseadh**, and yet I do not know a form **macht**, nor can I find one anywhere. **cadfarligettur** is *quem amiserunt*.

33 **an aithfeaghadh in begain bid** *in compensation for the small* (quantity) *of food*, but Latin is *in comparatione ad illam parvum cibum*.

Column 22.

1. **is usa linadh na dighe na linadh an bidh** This is one of the Aphorisms of Hippocrates, although the author does not mention it—eleventh of the Second Book—Ῥᾶον πληροῦσθαι ποτοῦ ἢ σιτιοῦ *facilius est repleri potu quam cibo*

LINE

4 **na biodh go gar do theine ocus na denuid coimhriachtain,** etc, I would translate this last word as *effort*, for the word and context would bear this rendering, but the Latin has it *nec igni nec coitu approximent*

14. This is a little troublesome **in t'errach a féil peaduir** *in the Spring at the feast of St Peter* The feast of Peter Apostle is 29th June. That of St. Patrick, 17th March, would fit rightly, but Patrick is never *Petrus* but *Patricius*

19 **doréir nan astroluighedh,** etc, *et hoc secundum Astronomos qui ponunt tempora aequalia—non sic Medici*

Observe the contraction for **noch,** l = *vel* = **no** + **c** with aspiration.

27 **fo examhlacht uairedh a laetheadh** *secundum horas diversas diei.*

30 **na h'uighi ocus a caibhdeal** *ova et candellum de ovis valent flebotomatis.* The Gaelic is evidently *made* from "candellum," which I cannot follow. That it was something *white* (from *candeo*) made from eggs is clear—custard pudding, or what we please

COLUMN 23

2. **in potaitsi . . . do cabhlan ocus do hocus,** etc., "fiat brodium de caulibus, malva, salvia, petrosilino vel de albis capitis porrorum decoctis et expressis" (1595).

6 **ocus a coimsuighedh le baindi almont** *and mingled with milk of almonds*, "cum lacte amygdalarum confectis"

7. **gurub romaith an t'Ord.** I prefer here to **an toradh** for it reads better with context, although the writing of the word favours the latter, and the grammatical setting is also in favour of it Latin, however, is *dico quod amygdalae comestae sicut sunt vel excorticate sunt optimi fructus flebotomatis et ethicis* [hecticis]

11 **lucht na ptisisi** *those of phthisis*—such as suffer from phthisis

23 **eanbruithi** *soup*, suggests that there is *a bird* in it, at any rate etymologically, for it is frequently written **énbhruithe** The Sc. Gaelic is **eanaraich** for *broth, soup*, but this would not greatly oppose my suggestion Cormac's Glossary says that it means *the water of flesh*, from old **en** water + **bruithe** *flesh*

32 **oir is dúintech righin iat** *for they are constringent and tough, quia est valde oppilativa et viscosa* **Treabhantar** is *curds and whey* (O'G) The Latin is *pinguedo lactis vel crema*

LINE

1. The plants named in this paragraph are—
"Kale" *Brassica oleracea*, **Ocus** *Oculus Christi* Wild Sage, *Salvia verbena* (but Lat. *malva* mallow), **Saithsi** sage, parsley, and the white heads of leeks—with milk of almonds.

2. Borrage, Bugloss *Echium vulgare*, Violet, Mercurial, Spinache, Monk's rhubarb *Rumex patientia*, Lettuce, the tops of Fennel, parsley and Avens *Geum urbanum* the "herb Bennet" *herba benedicta*, because, as Platearius says, the Devil cannot enter a house in which the root is kept.

Column 24

2. **na h'oisreaghdha** *the oysters* and the half-raw things are bad

4. **is beg nach leth don dileaghadh. cogaint maith in bídh** *good cooking of the food is nearly half of the digestion*—a very wise observation

9. I misread this sentence at first, and almost excusably, because of the peculiar use of the word **tindisnech**, and because of the miswritten **daniri** for **dan aire**. The meaning is that "those err who eat food *too hurriedly* or *ravenously*, for thus they sometimes eat injurious things without being brought *to their notice*"—*errant qui nimis festinantur comedunt et aliquando comedunt nociva et non advertunt.*

12 Here, as is usual, the coming new Chapter is announced—Of the Age and of the Complexion—no doubt also to save space

14 **daoine óga—sen-daoine—macaoimh**, although all Masculine in form, and literally, are nevertheless better rendered as *young adults, old people*, and *youths*

22 **caithid neithi seimhe . noc[h] intuighter go luath** *comedunt igitur subtilia quae cito convertantur.*

29 **bit tirim go foirimillach**, etc., *sunt sicca exterius et solidiora per totum ideo minus divisibilia a calore.*

Column 25

1. **is olc aran na pastae** *panis pastillorum est malus*, probably something of our own *past-ry*—**riaghail forlethon** *regula generalis*

4 **intan taidhillter e** *quum tangitur.*

LINE

7 **In t'aibstinens measardha is ro-árd in leighes e** *the moderate abstinence is very high healing*—it is a noble treatment This is one of the very many native, wise comments to be met in the Text, showing all the time that the author was thinking and writing upon the basis of a sound and observant experience *Abstinentia enim moderata est summa medicina.*

14 **is ro-urusa lis na sen-daoinibh in tréiginus d'fhulang** *old people bear emptiness* (abstinence) *very easily*

19 **is leor ansacht**, etc , *phlegmatici bene possunt jejunium*

20. **fiond** in MS should be **find**

24. **oir is luigha in tes disgaoiles indtu**, etc , *qui calor dispersus est minor et possunt plus resistere*

COLUMN 26

5. **nar bu dimaoin let céimniughadh déis na coda** *and do not think it is in vain to take a walk after the meal*—after the supper This is probably the source of the proverbial advice "After supper walk a mile," and see Introduction, p 12, "post coenam stabis aut passus mille meabis."

8 **na conaim ar th'fual ocus na héigin[i]gh go láidir do shuig[h]i** *do not restrain thy urine and do not distress thy seat*—the bowel. This is in effect the same advice as is given Col 14, 32, with perhaps the implied difference, or rather agreement, that restraining strongly, and forcing the bowel unnaturally, are both wrong and very injurious

12. **ataid naoi socamhuil do beir in fíon glan duit** *the clean* (pure) *wine will give thee nine comforts*—or benefits, namely

1. **imdaighi na brigha** *it will increase the powers* (the strength)
2. **lagaid na hinde línta** *it will relax the full intestines*
3. **nertaighi in gaili** *it will strengthen the stomach*
4. **ocus in incinn** *and it will strengthen the brain*
5. **do bir in croidhi subaltach** *it will give the merry heart*
6. **do ní dánacht** *it will make* (give) *courage—efficit audacem*
7. **togairmidh an t'allus** *it will call forth the sweat*
8. **geuraigi in t'indlecht** *it will sharpen the intellect—aptat ingenium*
9. **ocus do ní foirbheartas do na cáirdibh** *and it will make a stimulus to the friends*—towards friendship

This is a very fair statement and withal correct—and yet

LINE "let moderation be with it so that its working may not be perverted." The case for the use of wine could hardly be better stated.

25 The contraction which I have extended as **foirbheartas** (9 *supra*) O'G. renders as **forbfailtecus**, where **for** is an "extensive" + **failtecus** an *agreeable welcoming*, and O'R has **forbhfaoileadh** for *mirth* = **for** + **faoilidh** *joyful*. Latin is *tali lusus congaudat amico*.

31 **fhuar** MS should be **fhuair.**

Column 27

inté caithius cainel *he who uses cinnamon*—a very interesting expression which the modern language has lost. We cannot now say **intè** *the he* or *the him*, but we still retain **inté** *the she* or *the her*. Scottish Gaelic has lost the Masculine form but the Feminine remains.

Et is lór so, etc. This finishes the Tract. The rest is a postscript with no reference to the section of the *Rosa Anglica* upon which our Text is based.

It is difficult to say whether the handwriting of the rest of this Column is the same as that of the Text so far—although it almost certainly is, and therefore is that of Aodh O'Cendainn.

go h'ealadhanach le teine *per artificium, per ignem*.

Column 28

5. **Eochair gach uile eolais Ipocras,** *Hippocrates* (is) *the key of all knowledge*, was born in the island of Cos about 460 B.C. He was of the family of hereditary physicians descended from Aesculapius. His father Heraclides, himself a famous physician, taught him in his early days. After extensive travel and a wide experience, he established the great medical school of Cos, where he taught that the right conduct of life and right diet was the basis of health and the cure of all disease. His *Aphorisms*, which seem to have been culled from his extensive writings either by himself or by some of his followers, though fairly well known, but yet not so well known as they should be, are even now worthy of attention. Some sixty works are left us to his credit, but his authorship of several of these is doubtful. Galen (Col. 1, 6) was his great commentator. He is said to have died at Larissa in Thessaly B.C. 357.

COLUMN 29.

The few words here are of little interest except that "Donald MacBeath wrote this."

FURTHER NOTES.—I. **Sanis** *to the healthy* It is most interesting to notice how the significance of language changes. Our in-*sane* people now are out of their mind In the old time they were out of their health or *wholeness.* They were "broken" people. It is difficult to see the advance in conception Perhaps there is none The best definition of health that I ever learned was from the late Sir James Paget, if I am not mistaken, "If you close your eyes you don't know you are there at all" I have met with another definition in a margin of an old Latin text, "Qui bene ingerit, digerit, egerit is est sanus," but this reduces the human being to an animal machine pure and simple, and it is as well not to translate it into English, and certainly not into Gaelic, for the language is too plain It reminds us strongly of "Rob Donn's" famous and perfect definition of the "useless," **Ghineadh iad is rugadh iad is thogadh iad is dh'fhás; chaidh strác do'n t'saoghal thairis orr' 's mu dheireadh fhuair iad bás**

XII. 14. The following from Add 546, B M Fol 1 shows the distinction here made very clearly **Ata cuid do na leigheasuibh aenda ocus cuid ele comsuighithi** *some of the medicines are simple and others are compound.*

The **punctum delens** is often met with in these MSS Where the scribe, through carelessness or ignorance, has written a letter which should not be there, he or some one else on noticing the mistake put a dot *under* the letter It is seen under the first **n** of **ieinunius** VI 16, under **i** of **oire** XIX 12, and under **ac** at end of XXVIII 21

At XVI 31 observe **uair** in the margin and the mark of reference between **isí** and **is** therefore **isí uair is fearr**

GLOSSARY

A

A, An the Article *the*, **a samhrad ocus an geimhredh** *the summer and the winter* 21, **do lucht na h'eslainti** *to those of the ill-health* 1, **an gaili** *the stomach* 26 It is in frequently, **in foculso** *this word* 7, **in dieta** *the diet* 9

A for in mod. **an** *in*, **a caibidil comhartha na coimplex** *in the chapter upon the marks* (or signs) *of the complexion* 1, **a ceim ocus a foirm** *in degree and in form* 1, **a póiribh nam ball** *in the pores of the parts* or organs 11, **an aimsir asan** (for **ins an**) **dtaighter** *the time in which* 14, **a croccan** *into a pitcher* 8

A, As *out of, from*, Lat **ex**, Gk ἐξ **as a ghaili** *out of the stomach* 11

A *his, her, its*, **féttur a remh-choimhed** *it may be prevented* 2, **a aighiadh** *his face* 9, **a thráta Muiri** *his hours of Mary*, **in an dúsacht** *in their waking*—awake, in the day 1; **drong ele a gcinn ocus drong ele a gcnámha** *some people* (chose) *their heads and other people their bones* 18

Abair *say*, **mar an abair** *where he says* 2, **et dan abrairsi aburadh a thráta Muiri**, *let him say his hours of Mary*

Abfullan "**auellana**" *the hazel nuts* 19

Ac for **acht** *but*, **ac gurub lugha is fuar in t'iasg** *but that the fish is less cold* 18, **ach ar crichnughadh** *but after finishing* 19 It is for **ag** *at* Col 5 **ac ind aimsir** *at the time*

Adeir, adeirim, adeirimsi, adeirur 1, all are forms of the irregular verb to *say* as are **adeirit, adir** 2, **mar adeir Hali** *as Hali says* 1, **maseadh adeirim** *therefore I say* 1, **mar a deirur** *as is said* 1 **adeirimsi** *I myself say* 2, **adir Hali** *H says* 2, **adeirit drong** *some people say* 2 **mar a dubhurt Rufhus** *as R said* **mar a dubhramar** *as we said* 10

Adharc *horn* The word primarily means *the thing to defend with* but here it means the horn-cup used for "cupping"

The word had another side meaning as *trumpet* whence **gilla-adhairce** *horn-boy* or trumpeter, **dlighear an adharc do cur** *where the horn should be applied* 27

Adhbur *cause, reason*, **ocus is ar in adhbur sin** *and it is for that reason* 4

Ae *the liver*, **arson nan ae do beith faoi in ghaili** *because the liver* (lit *livers*) *is under the stomach*, **cum nan ae** *towards the livers* 13, **is na haeibh** *in the livers* 19

Aedaighi *clothes*, G **aodach; ocus cuiredh aedaighi go glan uime** *and let him put clean clothes upon him* 9 See **Edach.**

Aeir *air*, **droch aeir** *bad air* 13, **glantur an t-aer** *the air shall be cleansed* 27

Aforismorum is Latinised ἀφορισμῶν (of) *the Aphorisms*, **do aforismorum féin** *of his own Aphorisms* 20—and frequently.

Ag, *at*, **ag tuigsin in texasin** 2, **ag neach** *at a person* 10 It goes with the Infinitive, **ag iarraidh** *a-seeking*, **ag tuigsin** *understanding* 2, **ag ol** *a-drinking*, and with intervening pronoun **ag a losgadh** *burning it*, lit *at its burning* 12. **ag a caithimh** *eating it—at its eating* 10 It also enters into composition with the pers prons as **agam, agat, aige,** etc, **bith a fis aghutt** *let you understand* 23, **bith a fis agut** 23

Aghaidh, *face*, G **aghaidh** "in face of", **an aghaidh in rema fhuar** *against the cold rheum* 26, **an aghaidh gach uile eslainti** *against every disease* 27, **a lamha ocus a aighiadh** *his hands and his face* 9 **muna bia in gnathughadh ina aighidh** *if the habit be not against it* 14

Aháithle, *after*, **a h'áithle sin** *after that* 12, **d'áithle na cuislindi** *after the vein—letting* 21, **as a h'áithle** *after it* 8, **as a h'aithle sin** *after that* 9

Aibstinens, Lat **abstinentia,** Eng **abstinence**, **in t'aibstinens measurdha is ro-árd in leighes e** *the moderate abstinence is a very high cure* 25—an excellent cure

Aicidigi pl of **acaid** *a pain, dis-ease*, with the same original stem as **urchoid,** which see, **measruighter aicidigi na h'anma** *the diseases of the mind are to be here considered—*"measured" 13 Note under **Anum**

Aighchi, G **oidhche** *night*—see **oidchi** **salchur na h'aighchi** *the filth of the night* 27

Áil *will, desire, pleasure*, **madh áil let,** "si vis," *if you desire* 1, **madh áil let beith fallain** *if you wish to be healthy* 25.

Áilginach *easy, gentle*, **siubhul áilginach** *a gentle walk* 12

Aimsir *time, season*, W **amser**, Bret **amzer**, **tar an aimsir** *over* or *beyond the time* 5, **aimsir na h'eslainti** *the time of illness* 7; **an aimsir in geimridh . . . an aimsir an erraich** *in the season of winter in the season of spring* 16, **ag cinn aimsire** *at the end* (head) *of a time* 17, **a cinn moirain dh'aimsir** *at the end of a long time* 28

Aindeonach *unwilling, forcedly, compulsory* from **an** privative + **deonach** *desirous*, **gan fostogh ainndeonach** *without compulsory or forceful stopping*—of the breath 7

Ainmidhi, Adj *animal* from **ainmhidh** *animal, beast*, **ona ballaibh ainmidhi** *from the animal parts* 27 Compare **ballaibh spirutalta** *the spiritual parts*, four lines down **Lis in thochlughadh ainmidhe** *with the animal* (natural) *desire* 10, **na hainminnthibh caithid na daoine** *the animals that men eat* 19.

Ainnsein, **annsein**, **aindsein**, **aindhsein**, Mod **ansin** = **in** + **sin** *in that* time. **indarbadh ainnsein** *let him then expel* 9, **aindsein coimleadh an chorp** *and then let him rub his body* 9, **coimleadh aindhsein a fhiacla** *let him then rub his teeth* 9

Aire *heed, attention*. **ní éigin d'aire** *something of heed* 15, **tabhradh an aire riu** *let them take heed* 17, **tabhradh lucht an droch fhollamhnuighi an air riu** *let those of bad habit* (in diet) *beware* 17

Aireochuid from **airighim** *I feel*, G **fairich** *feel, perceive* **gin go n'airgid ar an lathair e aireochuid fós go maith** *yet though they do not feel it in their presence* (i e now) *they shall feel* (and know) *it too well*—later on 17

Airgid. See last

Áirighi and **áirighthe** *sure, especial*. **tinneas an cinn go h'áirighi** *the pain of the head especially* 27

Ais *back, backwards*, **dlighear a treorughadh tar a ais** *he must be led back*—to his first position 17 This phrase **tar a ais** is now in Sc Gaelic **air ais** See Note, Col 17

Aithfegadh *comparison*, O D, but in the text *compensation* would seem to be nearer the meaning as Col 21 **an aithfeaghadh in becain bídh** *in compensation for the small quantity of food*, and in Col 3 the meaning would seem to be nearly the same **an aithfheghadh coimplexa lenna**

dıubh (twıce) *ın compensatıon for black humors*—to make up for them

Aithi *proofs*, probably akın to G **aithne** *knowledge* "**co-gnosco**". **eolus ocus aithi báıs** *the knowledge and proofs of death* 28. **Aithaıdhim** *I know, perceıve*, G **fáth** *cause, reason* But see the versıon of the second post-scrıpt, p. 57, where the word ıs wrıtten **aithne.**

Allus *sweat, perspıratıon*, G **fallus**, **arson fuighill an alluis** *for the remaıns of the sweat* 9, **togairmidh an t'allus** *ıt will call forth the sweat* 26

Almont *almond*, **le baindı almont** *wıth mılk of almonds* 23 **ro-maıth an toradh na h'almoint** *the almonds are excellent fruıt* 23

Álucadh, G **adhlucadh** *ınterment, burıal*. **ocus d'órdaıgh a cur fo na cınn san alucadh** *and he ordered ıt to be put under hıs head ın the burıal* 28

Amach *out, wıthout, outsıde* The constructıon of the word ıs ınterestıng It lıterally means *ın the field* **in sa magh** and ıt ıs the opposıte of **Asteach** (whıch see) meanıng *ın the house.* Thıs ıs the "motıon' form **Amuıgh** ıs the "rest" form We say **tha e'dol amach** *he ıs goıng out*, but **tha e amuıgh** *he ıs out* The word ıs used ın the text very often as an "extensıve", **tar modh amach** *outsıde of the usual* 12 **osoın amach** *henceforth* 27

Amháin *only* for **na-n-má** essentıally meanıng *not more* **feoil amháın** *flesh* (meat) *only* **aran amháın** *bread only* 10 **én uair amháın** *once* (one tıme) *only* 20, **én dige amáın** *of one drınk only* 7

Amhlaidh *lıke as, so*, W. **amal**, Bret **evel**, Lat **sımil-ıs** ? **ocus ıs amhlaidh is follaine iat** *and so they are the more healthy* —broken ınto water, "poached" 22.

Anail, *the breath*, W **anal**, Corn. **anal**, Bret. **alan**, Sansk **anıla** *wınd*, Lat **anhelo** *I breathe*, **bıs an anail beg minıc** *the breath wıll be small* (feeble) *and frequent* 4 **gan claochlogh anala** *wıthout change of breath* 7

Anbhfhaine *weakness*, from **an** *very* + **fann** *faınt, weak* The word ıs wrıtten very ırregularly, **o anmhfaınne na brighi** *from weakness of the vıtalıty* 7 **o anmhfaınne an ghaıle** *from weakness of the stomach* 12 **gaili anmfann** *a weak stomach* 23

Andam *seldom*, '**raro**," G **aineamh**, **ainbhith** (Mb) *unusual* ıs

andam is athumulta an suiper gearr *the light supper rarely hurts* 14—see **Athumulta**

Angar *near, close by*, for **in + gar** *proximity*, **angar do beith asuighi** *nearly sitting up* 13, **tairngidh cuigi gach ní bis angar dó** *it will attract towards it everything that is near it* 9, **go gar do theine** *near to a fire* 22.

Anís *anise*, **do maratrum ocus d'anís** *of Marathrum and of Anise* 12, **Marathrum** μάραθρον is *fennel* The borrowed English word as **fineal** is several times met with

Ann *in it*, **is maith macoll do cur and** *it is well to put acens in it* 25 It is sometimes difficult to translate, as, **uair ann** *sometimes* 25, **bidh drong ann** *there are some* (people) 17.

Anntu, *in them* 26, **indtu** 25, **inntu**, 27.

Ansacht from **ansamh** *hard, difficult* G **annsa** *better liked*—borne, **is leór ansacht le lucht lenna fiond treighinus d'fulang** *it is very* (sufficiently) *difficult for those of white humors to bear emptiness*—or hunger 25

Anum *life*, W **enaid**, Corn **enef**, Bret **eneff**, Lat **anima**, Gr ἄνεμος *wind, breath*, **na neithibh bis gan anum** *the things that are without life* 2, **na neithibh ambí anum** *the things in which is life* 2. **aicidighi na h'anma** *troubles of the mind* 13. Note, Col 13

Anus from **anaim** *I stay, rest, remain*, G **fan**, **gurub sia anus and** *that it is six* (hours) *it remains*—in the stomach 11. **anus uair and** *that sometimes stays* 12, **anuid uair and** *they remain sometimes*—for eighteen hours 12, **aimsir anmhana in bídh** *the time of staying of the food*—in the stomach 11

Aois *age*, W **oes**, Lat **aetas**; **ocus aois ocus gnathughadh** *and age and custom*—or habit 3, **do leith na h'aoisi** *concerning the age* 15.

Aon *one*, W, Bret, Corn **un**, Lat **un-us**, **o aon gnodugh** *from* (any) *one cause* 16

Aonda *unified, simple, single*, **ocus ni go h'aonda** *and not singly* 3 "**Aonda** is the opposite of **cumusc**," O R It refers to things used as "simples" and not co-mixed or compounded.

Aontighius *conforms with, agrees* The verb is based upon **aon** *one*, therefore to *unify*, to bring into agreement, **an gnathughadh aontaighius leis na neithi nádurra** *the*

custom or practice *which agrees with natural things*—or conditions 17, **as seachrannach aontughadh na meisg aon uair is in mí** *it is wrong to assent to* (the getting) *drunkenness one time in a month* 5

Aotrom is **an + trom** *unheavy* therefore *light* It is **édrom** and **édrum** in the same Col 14 The form given first is that of the present Sc Gaelic **In suiper gerr no édrom** *the short or light supper.*

Aphoplexia—see Note, Col 20

Ar has several values, all arising from the fact that the modern form embodies three old forms of different meaning and grammatical conduct **arson** *for the reason, for* the *sake* of, **arson fuighill an alluis** *for* (because of) *the remnant of the sweat* 9, **ar egla** *for fear* 13, **ar aon bórd** *upon one table* 10, 12, **ar in taobh ndes** *upon the right side* 13, **ar in camra** *upon the "stool"* 15, **ar dtuitim an bídh** *after the food has fallen* 8 In the old language it is often used in the sense of *against*, as here, **ar eslaintibh in t'samhruigh** *against the illnesses of summer* 21, **ocus coimheduigh ar truailledh na lenna** *and it will prevent the corruption of the humors*—against the corruption 26

Ára *kidney*, pl. **árann**, W **aren**, Lat **nefrones**, Gk νεφρὸς, **itir na h'airnibh** *between the kidneys* 27

Aran *bread*, same root as **ar-bhar** *corn*, Gk ἄρ-τος, Lat **arvum** *a field*, **aran amháin** *bread alone* 10, **na neithi beirbtur an aran** *the things cooked in bread* 24-25 **is olc aran na pastae** *the pastry bread is bad*—**panis pastillorum**

Árd *high*, akin Lat **arduus** and Gk ὀρθός, **le neithibh tesaighi, tirma, arda** *with things hot, dry and high* 3; **ocus bith in cend go h'árd** *and let the head be high*—well raised 13, **in t'aibstinens measurdha is ro-ard in leighes e** *the moderate abstinence is very high healing*—excellent treatment 25, **an inaduibh árda** *in high places*—on high ground 9, **do réir áirde** *according to height* 17

Argamainti (mar) *as argument*, very likely from English use of Lat **argumentum; do níter mar argamainti** *it is made* (or put forth) *as an argument*—or as reason 7.

Arís *again*, mod **arithist** for old **ar + frith + st** **Frith** is the mod prep **ri** in which the old and essential idea of *again-st* remains, **do geinemuin fhola arís** *to make blood again* 21

Arrsaidh *old, aged*, **ponair na pís úr na áirsaidh** *beans or* *peas, new* or *old* 23, **intan is áirsuigh an ré** *when the moon is old* 21, **mad ársaigh e** *if he is old*, whence **arrsuigecht** *agedness* 25

Artús *at first, in the beginning* **ar** *upon* + **tús** *beginning*, **sínedh artús a lamha** *let him stretch at first his hands* 9, **ocus mar aduburt artús** *and as was said at the beginning* 3

Asteach *inwards, within*, **ar egla droch aeir do dul asteach** *for fear of bad air going inside* **Isteach** is really a phrase **is** + **teach** for **ins in teach** *in the house, within*, as against **amach** *in the field, without*—which see

Astroluigedh *astrologers*, **do réir nan astroluighedh** *according to the astrologers* 22.

Ata *there is*, **Ataid** *there are*, **na togra ata aige** *the disposition which he has* 1, **ataid trí gneithi** *there are three kinds*—or ways 1, **trath ata sa bél** *while it is in the mouth* 8, **mar ataid na siriopighi** *as are* (such as) *the syrups* 8, **ata in croicind** *the skin is* 9, **ataitt moran** *there are many* 14

Athair *father*, Lat **pater**, Gr πατήρ—interesting as showing the loss of *p* in Gaelic, **a athaír fen** *his own father* 18.

Athnuaightech *renewing, restorative*, from **ath-** *re* + **nua** *new*, **dlighider an diet bith athnuaightech** *the diet should be restorative* 24.

Athumulta "molesta" Note, Col 14

Aturra mod **eatorra** the plural prep pron *between them*, **aturra ocus an gaile** *between them and the stomach* 8

Aueroys *Averrhoes*—see Note, Col 1.

Auicina *Avicenna*—see Note, Col 1.

B

Baindi *milk*, **baindi ocus iasg . . na fín ocus baindi** *milk and fish or wine and milk* 12, **baindi almont** *milk of almonds* 23, **bainne goirt sa t'shamradh** *sour milk* (i e butter-milk) *in the summer* 23, **uachtur baindi** *the upper-part of milk*, that is *cream* 23

Ball *limb, member, part*, **ona ballaibh spirutalta** *from the spiritual parts*—from "the higher centres" Compare this with the *Animal parts*, under **Ainmhidi**; **gidhedh is usa na boill ele do dileaghadh** *yet it is easier to digest the other parts* 18

Bás *death*, **eolus ocus áithi bais** 28—see **Aithi.**

Basilica *the basilic vein*—on the inside of the upper arm, **na cuislidhi renabur basilica** *the vein called Basilic* 27

Beagan *a little*, from **beag** *small, little*, **ocus dlighitt beagan do caithimh go minic** *and it is meet to use a little often* 24, **in begain bídh** *the small quantity of food* 21—see **Beg**

Beg *little*, G **beag**, W **bach**, Corn **bech-an**, Bret **bich-an**, so G **beagan**, **dlighitt began d'ól** *a little should be drunk* 21, **ocus uime sin is beg nach let[h] don dileaghadh .. cogaint maith in bidh** *and therefore it is but little* (very nearly) *that the half of the digestion is not in the good cooking* 24

Beir *give, bring*, **do beradh siubhal ar in mbiadh** *the food is put in motion* 8, **do beradh ar snàmh e** *it is set aswim* 8

Berbadh *a boiling*, **ar nam berbadh** *after being boiled* 23, from **berbaim** *I boil, seethe*

Betha *life*, **ina bhetha** *in* (*his*) *life* 18, **in betha degindaigh** *the later life*—or the end of life 28, **gach ní ina fuil betha** *everything in which is life* 3

Biadh *food*, W **bywyd**, Corn **buit**, Bret **boed** the same base throughout as in **Beatha** *life* and **Beo** *living*, **no go tuitim an biadh is an ghaile** *until the food has fallen from the stomach* 6

Blas *taste*, **oir is e in ní is fearr blas is ferr oilius** *for it is the thing of best taste that best nourishes* 19 **blas an bidh** *the taste of the food* 5

Bliadhna. Gen of **Bliadhan** *a year*, **aimsir na bliadhna** *the time of year* 3, **fa-cheithir sa bliadhain** *four times a year* 20, **én uair amhain acind a treas fithitt bliadhan** *once only* (a year) *at the end of three score years* 20

Bog *soft, tender* **na neithi maotha no boga** *the young and tender things* 24

Bolais *bullace* **nad bolais umorro ocus na risinedha** *but the bullaces and the raisins* 18

Borsaitsi *borage*, **potaitsi do borrsaitsi** *a pottage of Borage* The made Gaelic is not euphonious—nor is the English

Bradan *salmon*, **do tharr in bradain** *as regards the belly of the salmon* 19

Bráighedh *the chest, lungs, thorax*, lit the upper part, "the brae" It occurs in place-names as Brae, Braid (for **bra-**

ghad), na sróna ocus na bráighedh *of the nose and the lungs*—the chest 9.

Brég *a lie* G. **breug; ocus is brég sin** *and that is a lie* 2, **gidhedh is brégach na fersadha eile** *nevertheless the other verses lie* 22

Briala—briala d'ól *to drink a Briala.* The explanation is given lower down in the same Col 7 *Et* **iseadh tuigim trid in foculso briala i. in meid doghebadh nech gan claochlogh anala** *as much as a person gets without changing* (*i e* drawing) *breath.*

Brigh has an exceedingly wide range of meanings, all however agreeing in "the essence" Perhaps *strength* is the best single word to use for it. We say **brigh an sgeoil** *the "essence" of the tale,* **brigh an fhocail** the essential force or power of the word, **brigh an eorna** the essential strength or product of barley, that is, alcohol or whiskey, **obair gun bhrigh** a work without result, **ní gun bhrigh** a thing without sense or strength, **chaill se a bhrigh** he or it has lost its "strength," etc It is used in this text almost always for *strength,* **imdaighi na brigha** "mes multiplicat" 26

Brotha, **broth** *an eruption, the itch*, **anaighi . brotha na sliastadh ocus brotha in cuirp go h'uilidhi** *against eruptions of the thigh and eruptions of the body generally* 27

Brúchtaigh *belch, eructate*, **ac ind aimsir ar in mbruchtaigh** *in the time when he belches* 5

Buain *reap, cut, remove*, **a croicind do buain dibh** *their skins being cut away or taken off* 23

Buglosa *bugloss*, **do borrsaitsi ocus do buglosa** *of borage and bugloss* 23 Lat **buglossa,** Gr $\beta o\acute{v}\gamma\lambda\omega\sigma\sigma o\varsigma$

Buidhe *yellow*, **croicinn an ubhaill buidhe** *the skin of the yellow apple* 9

Bunuibh Dat pl of **Bun** *a foundation*, the lowest part of the trunk of a tree, the part next the trunk of the body from which a limb or a member or organ grows, as here, **bunuibh an righthigh (ruighe** *the forearm*), that is, *the elbows* 27.

C

Caban *a cavity, hollow* (O D), **na cabain inmhedhonach** *the internal cavities* 15

Caibidil *chapter*, Lat **capitulum; mar a deir Auıcına a caibidıl comhartha na coimplex** *as says Avicenna in the chapter upon the symptoms of the complexion*—or general health 1

Cáil *appetite*, **cáil ocus caındıghecht ocus órd ocus aımsir. ocus aoıs** *appetite and quantity and manner and time* (season) *and age* 3.

Caindighecht *quantity* The Gaelic and the English seem closely related. **Tabhaır an bıadh a gcaınndighect bıg** *give the food in small quantity* 16

Cainel *cinnamon*, Gr κιννάμωμον, **inté caithes caınel go mınıc** *the person who uses cinnamon frequently* 27

Cáirdibh Dat pl of **caraıd** *a friend* **ocus do ni foırbheartas do na cáırdıbh** *and it will make assistance to the friends*—it is a great help to friendship 26

Cáisi *cheese*, from Lat **caseus**, W **caws**, Bret **kaouz; seachnadh cáısı antán sın** *avoid cheese in that time* 22

Caithim *I eat, use, wear*, **goraıbhi a athair fén cét bhadhan ina bhetha arson nar chaıth toırrthı** *that his own father was a hundred years in his life because he did not indulge in fruit* 18, see under **Cainel** 27. **ıntán caıthıus nech bıadha urchoideacha** *when a person eats hurtful foods* 12, **caıthme ın bıdh** *the use or usage of food* 9 **ıs cum beıth am bethaıdh caithım ocus nı cum caıthme bım am betaigh** *it is that I may be in life I eat and not to eat that I am in life* 25

Camra *stool, seat*, **Camera?**, **nach maıth beıth gu ro-fadha ar ın camra** *that it is not well to be too long on the stool* 15

Caninus *dog-ish*. **ocus gan urlugadh na apıtıtus caınınus and** *without vomiting or dog-appetite*—**bulımıa** 5

Canoin *a Canon, rule*, **adeır Galen sa canoınsı** *G says in this canon* 16 The word comes from Gk κάνων through Latin It primarily meant a stick, a "cane," hence a "ruler," whence a *rule* or *doctrine* It has been confused with G **cánaın** *speech, language*, but the words are in no way related This latter is simply **canamhuın** *language*, from **can** *say, speak*, which we have in **caınnt** *speech* also

Caomhna from **caomhnaım** *I spare, save, restrict*, G **caomhaın**, **dlıghi ın duıne égnaidhı a caomhna feın** *the wise man should restrict himself* 6

Cara *a friend, relative*, here used adjectively, **gurub mó ıs**

cara don nadur fuil derg *that red blood is more near to* (the) *nature* 20

Cas Lat **casus**, Eng *case* In mod Gaelic the word means *a difficulty*, **ocus is mar sin sa cás so** *and so it is in this case* 2

Cathaighim *I fight, defend*, **oir cathaighidh re gach h'uili truailledh** *it will defend against every pollution* 18

Ceathardha *the fourth*, G. **ceathramh**, Lat **quartus**, *from* **ceathair** *four*, W. **pedwar**, Corn **peovar**, Bret **pevar**, Lat **quatuor**, Gk τέτταρες, Goth **fidvor**—interesting as showing the letter-change in the different languages, **in ceathardha inadh** *the fourth place* 27.

Céimniuughadh, base **céim** *a step*. "make a step," take a walk, **ocus nar bu dímaoin let ceimniughadh deis na coda** *and do not let it be foolishness to you to walk after the meal* 26.

Cena *yet, already*, **gidhegh cena** *nevertheless yet* 3

Cennduibh Dat pl of **ceann** *head*. **no do cennduibh geala losa** *or of white heads of leeks* 23—**de albis capitis porrorum**

Cephalica the vein called *Cephalic* This is on the outside frontal at the elbow, and the Basilic on the inside—of the upper arm—take up all the superficial veins of the fore-arm, **na cuislinn ren aburthar sefalica** *the vein to which is said* (named) *cephalic* 27

Certuighter from **ceartaighim** *I correct, adjust, put right*, **go certuighter e arna mhárach** *that it shall be put right on the morrow* 11, **ni certaighter sa dara dileaghadh** *it shall not be put right in the second digestion* 4

Cét *a hundred* W. **cant**, Corn **cans**, Bret **kant**, Lat **cent-um**; **goraibhi a athair fén cét bliadhan ina bhetha** *that his own father was a hundred years in his life* 18

Cét *the first*, **sa cét partegul** *in the first (p)article* 25 This word has no philological kinship with **cét** *a hundred*—so far as can be yet seen **Cétna** in the phrase **mar an cétna** *likewise* is from this source, **et mar in cétna** *and so likewise* 25 **a cét oir** (for **uair**) **deis a dhenta** *the first time after its being done* 17, **nach denonn dighultus a cét oi** (for **an cét uair**) *that he makes not revenge the first time* 17. **in cét dileaghtha** *the first digestion* 9 **sa cét leabur** *in the first book* 9.

Cétfadhuibh *the senses*—the seat of the *first impressions*—a very good word

Ceum *a step, degree*, **ocus nı do réır ceıme** *and not according to degree* 1

Cinnamomo (**de**) *of cinnamon* 27

Cindtı *sure, reliable* **o leitreachuıbh cindtı** *from reliable letters* (or writings) 9

Cinn, ceann *a head, end* W **pen,** Bret. **penn**—which shows the change of **c (k)** and **p** in the two branches of the Keltic speech, **drong ele a gcinn ocus drong ele a gcnámha** *some* (people) *their heads and other people their bones* 18 **ocus a cinn morain dh'aımsır** *and at the end of a great length of time* 28 **d'ordaıgh a cur fona cınn** *he ordered it to be put under his head* 28, **ag cınn aımsıre** *at the end of a time*—after a long time 17, **acınd a dara fithett blıadhan** *at the end of the second twenty years*, i e. fortieth 20

Cıreadh *let him comb* **círeadh a chend** *let him comb his head* 9 The base is **cír** *a comb.*

Cithfighter from **chí** *I see* **mar do císthfighter** *as may be seen* 5.

Clais *a furrow, ditch, hollow*, W **claıs**, **a clais cuıl ın cinn** *in the hollow of the back of the head* 27

Claochladh *alteration, change*, G **caochladh** *a change* **gan claochlogh do beıth ar ın fual** *without change being upon the urine* 4 **an deoch claochluıghtech "potus alteratıvus"** *the alterative drink* 8 **gan claoghlogh anala** *without changing of breath* 7

Claonas and **Claonadh** *inclines, inclination* **ın corp claonas do claonadh nadurdha** *the body that inclines* (that way) *of natural disposition* 1

Clé *left* (hand), G **clí**, W **cled**, Bret **kleız**; **ocus na lamha clé san fogmhur** *and the left hands in autumn* 21

Cloch *a stone*, G **clach**, W **clwg**, **no cloch no ydorıpıs** *nor stone* (in the bladder) *nor dropsy* 14

Cluas *the ear*, W **clust**, O Sax **hlust**, Eng *listen*, **ocus siasanach isna cluasaıbh** *and noise or humming in the ears* 14

Cluthur, clúdhaım *I cover*, G **clúthaıch** *cover, shelter*, **ocus cluthur le h'édach gomaith e** *and let him be well protected with clothes*—covering 13

Cnamha pl of **cnamh** *a bone* **drong ele a gcınn ocus drong**

ele (a) a gcnamha *one class* (of people) *their heads and another class their bones* 18

Cnaoi from **cnaoidhim** *I consume, spend*, **arna cnaoi ocus arna dísgaoilidh** *spent and scattered* 16, **an droing bhis arna cnaoi** *those who are wasted* 23

Cno *a nut, the hazel nut*, **gidhedh a deirim do na cnóib** *yet I say regarding the nuts* 19 **abair gurab fallain na cnó do sír do na haeibh "dic auellanas epati semper fore sanas"** *say that the nuts are healthy always to the livers* 19

Coctana *a small Syrian fig*, Gk κόταννα, **mar ataid péredha ocus coctana** *as are pears and coctanas* 18

Coda Gen of **cuid** *a portion, a meal*, **is olc . goluath déis na coda** *it is bad too soon after the meal* 12, **ar deiredh na coda** *at the end of the meal* 25, **na sa cuid ele dhe** *than in the other portion of it* 18

Codladh *sleep*, from **codlaim** *I sleep* **atháili sin codladh go measarrdha** *after that sleep moderately* 12, **do nít daoine imdha lá don oidchi** *many men make a day of the night* 13, **ocus fós gan nemh-codlaidh do beith air** *and still without insomnia being upon him* 5

Coidigenn from **cuidighim** *I keep, assist* **is mór coidigenn in baindi don gaili fuar** *the milk greatly helps the cold stomach* 23

Coigill Imper of **coigilim** *I spare* **coigill fíon** *spare wine* **"parce mero." Merum** is wine unmixed with water, an intemperate form of drinking—so Horace uses the word 26

Coimed *looking, watching, warding*, **"conseruatiuum,"** G **coimhead, rem-coimed** *fore-seeing, fore-watching* **"pre-serua-tiuum", mad áil let an coimplex . do coimet** *if you desire to retain the complexion*—that is the full health 1, **preseruatiuum** *that is*, the *fore-seeing* 1 **dlighear an gnathughadh do coimet** *the* (ordinary) *habit* or custom *should be observed* 5

Coimhéigniughadh *forcing, restraining*. **gan coimhéigniugh-adh** *without restraining*—the breath 7

Coimheduighi, a later way of writing **Coimet,** as Col 1 **ocus coimheduighi ar truailledh na leanna** *and it will prevent the corruption of the humors* 26

Coimleadh from **comlaim** *I rub*, W Likely **co + melim** Lat **molo** *I grind, rub* **ocus coimleadh an corp** *and let him well-rub the body* 9 *Rub* for same is used of the teeth 9

Coimint, *comment,* Lat. **commentatio** *reflection, thought*, **sa seathadh coimint** *in the sixth Comment* 1

Coimplex *complexion, the general full health,* see **coimed,** and Note, Col. 1

Coimriachtachain *want, distress, hard labour,* lit. *over-reaching*, **ocus na dénaid coimhriachtain** *and let them not over-work* 22, **an drong lerbáil coimhriachtachain do gnathughadh** *those who would wish to practise co-reaching*, **gidhedh is brégach na fersadha eile chuireter... ar in coimhriachtain** *nevertheless they are lying those other verses that would put a person to co-reaching*—after a meal 22.

Coimsuighedh from **comhsuidighim** *I compound, mix* (O'D), **ocus a coimsuighedh le baindi almont** *and mixed with milk of almond* 23

Cóir *just, right* = "**co-vero,**" **co-fíor; do budh cóir** *it was right* 10

Collegett, sa cuigedh leabur do collegett *in the fifth book of Colliget* 2—Note, Col 2.

Coithcenn *common, customary* **gidhedh ata in gnáthughadh coitcind ina aighidh so** *nevertheless the ordinary custom* (or practice) *is against this* 18

Colpaid *the calf of the leg,* G **calpa; ar làr na colpaid** *on the flat of the calf* 27

Comentator (Damascenus) See Note, Col 3

Comfhurtacht *comfort, relief* **ocus do ni comfhurtacht an disnía ocus an asma** *and it will make comfort* (to—will relieve) *the dispnoea and the asthma* 27

Comhartha *a sign, proof* **et is e is comurtha** *and it is a sign* 4. **comhurthaighi eile** *other proofs* 4. **a caibidil comhartha na coimplex** *in the chapter* (upon) *the signs of general health* 1

Comnuighi *dwelling, remaining* **a comnuighi sa corp** *remaining in the body* 11

Comuisgim *I mix*. **ocus tic de sin go comuisgter ris e** *and it comes of that that the one is mixed with the other* 10

Congmhail, congmhailim *I hold, retain* **arna congmhail sa bhél** *after being held in the mouth* 9 **ydoripis o chongbail an fuail** *hydropsy from retention of the urine* 14

Connmhain from **congbhaighim** *I hold, retain,* G **cumail,** Irish **congmhail** also. **arson go connmhain an tes nádura** *because the natural heat is retained* 13 **na neithi rós-**

tuighthi connaımhter tar oidchi *the roasted things that are kept over night* 25, **na conaim ar th'fual** *retain not thy urine* 26.

Continoidech *continent*, **an caindıghecht continoidech do médughadh** *to increase the ordinary quantity*, 8

Contrardha *the contrary*, **sa taobh contrardha** *on the opposite side*—or against this 3 This word is very often, and very neatly, written by a ɔ—a c inverted with a superscript. It is *e contrario* 11

Corp *the body*, Lat **corpus**, W **corff**, Bret. **corf**; **don corp mesardha** *to the temperate* (abstemious) *body* 1, **an corp uili** *the whole body* 19, **na cuırp theo. . ocus na cuırp fhuara** *the warm bodies. . and the cold bodies* 3

Cosaibh Dat pl of **cos** *a foot*, G **cas**; **ocus folmuıghi ona cosaıb** *and it will empty*, or draw from, *the feet* 28

Cosmhaile from **co + samhail** *co-similar*, *alike* · **o neıthibh cosmhaile do níter in coimed** *from similar things prevention is made* 1, **cona cosmuılıbh**, *with the like*—things 23, **tabhair neithi cosmuile** *give similar things* 1, **do tharr in bradain ocus da cosmailibh** *as regards the belly of the salmon and similar things* 19.

Creit *believe*, "**crede profanum ırasci**", **creit gurub dímaoın duıt ferg do denamh** *believe that it is vain for thee to make anger* 25.

Críchnughadh *ending, finishing*, **ar críchnughadh an cét dileaghtha** *after finishing the first digestion* 19

Croccan dım of **croc**, G. **crog** *a pitcher, an earthen vessel*, **croccan fhiuchach** *a boiling earthen vessel* 8.

Croicend *a skin*, G **craıcıonn**; **no a croıcınd do buaın dibh** *or their skins to be reaped* (taken) *of them* 23, **croıcinn an ubhaill buidhe** *the skin of the yellow apple* 9

Croidhi *the heart*, G. **cridhe**, W. **craıdd**, Lat **cor, cordis**, Gk **καρδία**, **ocus do bır in croıdhı subaltach** *and it will give the merry heart* 26

Cruadi pl. of **cruaidh** *hard, dry*, **ocus neithı cruaidi** *and hard* or dry *things*, 24

Cuala *heard*, **mar do chuala o daoinibh fírindecha** *as I have heard from truthful men* 12.

Cudrumacht *heaviness, weight* for **con + trom** "co-heavy" **na daıne dambia cudrumacht** *the men* (or those) *to whom there is heaviness* 19 **go comhtrom** *evenly* 11 **dambıa**

cudrumacht eli ann *if there is other evenness*—"**ceteris paribus**" 19

Cugat *towards* or *to thee.* The prep **gu** older **cu** is here repeated and the **t** is the second personal ending for **tu** *thou* Scottish Gaelic writes **thugad**, but this is etymologically wrong, **in coimplex dogabuis cugat** *the general health which thou hast taken to thee* 1, **nach gabann nignim cuige** *that he will not suffer from inaction* 1.

Cuigedh from **cuig** *five*, G **cóig**, W. **pump, pimp**, Corn. **pymp**, Bret **pemp**, Goth **fimf**, Lat **quinque**, Gr **πέντε**—quite a lesson in consonantal change between the languages, **in cuigedh inadh** *the fifth place* or position 27

Cuimin the herb *cummin*, Gr **κύμινον**; **na caittir i acht maille cuimin** *let it not be used but along with cummin* 23, **maille saland ocus re cuimin** *along with salt and with cummin* 23

Cuimne *remembrance*, **ocus truaillidh in cuimne** *and it will corrupt the memory* 21.

Cumdaidh *shapen* The phrase is based upon the English, **bogsa cumdaidh** *a shapen box, a casket* 28

Cuir *put*, **cuiridh na suile an doimne ro-mór** *it will put the eyes in very great depth* 19, **dlighear an adharc do cur** *where the horn* ("cup") *should be put* 28

Cúirrenecht *spasms, cramps*, **gan cuirrineacht na gaothmairecht**, *without cramps or flatulence* 5

Cúis *a cause*, **ocus is cúis sin don mhorgadh** *and that is a cause of corruption* 4

Cuisighim *I cause, induce*, **cúisighind an cuisli ro-minic aphoplexia** *the frequent blood-letting will cause apoplexy* 20

Cuislind Gen of **cuisle** *a vein* The difference of vein and artery is never clear in this text **Is e folmughadh na cuislinne is mó anmfhainighius in brigh**, *it is the emptying of the vein that most weakens the strength* 20, **a caibidil na cuislinne** *in the chapter upon the vein* or blood-letting 20, **don cuislind, umorro,** *but regarding the vein*, that is, blood-letting 20 **Cuisle** is frequently used alone for blood-letting

Cúl *the back part of anything*, W **cil**, Corn **chil**, Bret **kil**; **a clais cuil in cinn** *in the hollow of the back of the head* 27

Cumdach *a covering*, **ocus cumdach orra** *and a covering upon them* 25 G. **comhdach**

Cumgaighind **cumhaingim** *I make narrow*, G **cumhang**

narrow, **arson go cumhgaighind an gaile ar in sgairt** *because the stomach closes upon* or presses on *the diaphragm* 4

Cumsanadh *resting, in tranquillity*, **ocus e a cumsanadh** *and he a-resting* 20.

D

Daingen *strong, tight*, **ocus is daingne go huilidhi iad** *for they are all stronger*, **ocus dainighter doréir dherbhtha ocus gnaithighi e** *and it is confirmed according to proofs and custom* 9.

Dallaidh *will blind*, **oir dallaidh sin nech** *for that will blind a person* 21. This is from Adj. **dall** blind, Corn. **dal**, W **dal**, Bret. **dall**.

Dánacht *boldness, courage*, **ocus do ní dánacht . . ocus geuraigi in t'indlecht** *and it will make courage . . and it will sharpen the intellect* 26

Daoinibh Dat. pl of **duine** *a man*, **o daoinibh fírindecha** *from truthful men* 12, Adj **in corp ndaonda** *the human body* 3, **na sen-daoine** *the old men* 25

Dara *second*, the other of two, from **ind + araile** *the other*, **in dara inadh** *the second position* 27.

Dealachadh *separating, separation*, from **delaighim** *I separate*, **do denadh dealughaidh atturra** *to make separation between them* 8

Dearbhadh *proof, confirmation*, base **dearbh** *certain, true* **doréir dhearbhtha** *according to proofs* 9

Deathach *smoke, vapour, fumes*, **na dhetaighi inmolta** *in offensive vapours* 5, but see Note

Dechra *difficult*, from **dí + cor** *difficult position* **Sochair** is *good position*, **dochair** is *bad position*, **dichair** is *no position* at all—a defect **is deachra an dealachadh on tes** *it is difficult to separate them from the heat* 24

Degh, G **deagh** *good*, W **da**, Cor **da**, Lat **dex-ter**, Gk. δεξιός *right*—see **deghbaladh**

Deghbaladh seems for **dég + boladh** *sweet* or *sweet-smelling*, **gnathaighter in cainel go minic or do bir an bél do deghbalaidh** *let cinnamon be used frequently for it will bring the mouth to sweetness* 26, **began d'fhín deghbalaidh** *a little of sweet wine* 5.

Deighinech *finally, at the end* **o ibhter an fion uair and go**

deighinech *since wine is drunk, time in*—and out (*i.e.* occasionally) *at the end* **in deoch ibhter go deighinech** *the drink that is drunk finally*—gives many pains 26—a bit of human experience

Deir *says*, **oir a deir Auicina** *for Avicenna says* 9, and frequent. Other parts of this Irregular Verb **Abair** *say*, meet us constantly, **mar an abair** *where he says* 5, **mar a dubhrumar roimhainn** *as we have said before* (us) 10.

Deiredh *the end*, **ar deiredh na coda** *at the end of the meal* 25. **Cuid** which means *a portion* seems to mean a meal always in the text It is interesting that **cuideachd** *a company* is the people who *share* with you what you have to give Our proverb says **Is moide cuid a roinn** *a portion* or a meal *is bigger for being shared.*

Deisgribhidech written wrongly for **deiscreidech** *discreet*, **duine ro-dheisgribhidech** *a very discreet man* 6.

Denom, G **denamh** *to do*, **ni h'urusa sin do denamh** *that is not easy to do* 10, **gurub dimaoin duit ferg do denamh** *that it is foolishness of thee to make wrath*—to get angry 25

Deoch *a drink*, **an deoch ibhter** *the drink that is drunk* 26, **is hégin gurob taréis an caithmhe ibhus nech deoch** *it is right* (necessary) *that it is after consumption* (after eating) *a person should drink a drink* 6, and not at the time of eating, **adeirim go fuilit tri deocha and** *I say that there are three drinks* 8

Dermair *intense, great*, **caoinedh dermair** *intense weeping* 16

Derna is frequently used for **deanadh** *to make or cause*, **ocus nach derna én urchoid doibh** *and that not one hurt comes to them* 8 **dan dernadh dia dighultus** *if God made revenge* 8.

Des, G **deas** *right* (hand), Lat **dexter**, W **dehen**, Corn **dyghow**, **na lamha desa san errach** *the right hands in the spring* 21, **ar in taobh ndes** *on the right side* 13

Diaigh *end* **na diaigh sin** *after that* end or time. G **na dheidh sin** and **an deigh sin** *after that* This is clearly the stem in **Deighinech**, which see **A cinn moirain dh'aimsir na diaigh sin** *at the end of a long time after that* 28.

Dibenta "in extremis" **Dibne** is *extremity*—of exhaustion, **oir bidh an drong sin dibenta** *for such people are exhausted* 6.

Diet *diet, nourishment.* Sc. G uses **diata** for "*a meal*", **ocus diet mesurdha** *and a moderate* (measured) *diet* 14

Dighe as Gen of **deoch** *a drink*, **ocus na caitter e déis dighi** *and let it be not used* (or *taken*) *after a drink, i e.* butter 23

Digultus *revenge, retribution*, **dan derna dia digultus,** *if God made retribution* 8

Dileaghaim *I digest*—food, **is usa na boill eile do dileaghadh** *it is easier to digest the other parts* 18, and in constant use throughout the text.

Dimaoin from **dí + maoin** "office-less" *in vain*, **ocus creit gurub dimaoin duit ferg do denamh** *for, believe that it is vain for thee to make anger*—to get wrathful 25, **ocus nar bu dimaoin let** *and it would not be wrong* (in vain) *of you*—to step out—after the meal 26.

Dimaoinus is the Abstract Noun from **dímaoin,** that is *foolishness, uselessness*, **oir teid an dimaoinus gach ní dibh so an égmais in misuir** *for all of these things go into uselessness* (are no use) *without the moderation* 26

Dirradas seems here to mean *a will* or *direction* It occurs three times in this postscript 28, where it can only have this meaning. The base is **dír, díor** *proper, right, lawful,* which occurs several times in *Cormac's Glossary*

Disgaolim *I dissolve, scatter*, for **dí + sgaoil + im; is luigha in tes di-sgaoileas indtu** *for the heat is less that is set free in them* 25.

Disnía for dispnœa, *difficult breathing* **an disnía ocus an asma** *the dispnœa and the asthma* 27

Diureticech *diuretic*, **na én ní diureticech** *nor one thing* (anything) *diuretic* 12.

Dlighim *I ought, have a right, it is a duty* Forms of this verb occur so often that quotation is not necessary The translation will sufficiently show its usage

Dlistinach *lawful, dutiful, right* G **dleasnach** of same force This is from a form **dligheas** *I ought,* with root **dligh** *a debt* or *right* Welsh **dled,** and Breton **dle,** of same meaning, **go dlistinach** *rightly* 4, **a meid andlistinaigh** *in unright, unreasonable quantity* 4

Doimne *depth,* an Abstract Noun from **domhann,** G **domhain** *deep* Welsh **dwfn** *and* Breton **don; oir cuiridh na súile an doimne ro-mór** *for it will put the eyes into a very great depth*—it will cause them to sink in their sockets 19

Drageta, a kind of comfit in which the drug is covered by sugar, chocolate, or gelatine It is the Fr. **Dragée** of the present day

Dragma, the Gk. *δραχμή* used here in quite the modern sense of sixty minims or three scruples 28.

Droch *bad, evil,* W **drwg,** Corn. **drog** Like a few other old Adjectives it always stands before the Noun as **droch-dhuine** *a bad man,* **droch-bheairt** *an evil deed*, **na h'éin do niter do droch róstadh** *the birds that are badly roasted* 24, **lucht an droch fhollamhnuighi** *those of bad rule* or evil conduct 17

Drong *a people, certain people,* of same meaning and perhaps of the same origin as G **dream** akin to Gk *δράγμα a handful* —of people, **bidh drong ann.. ocus drong ele. . ocus drong ele** *there are some people ..and other people and others* 18.

Duibh Gen of **dubh** *black* **lucht lenna duibh** *those of black humors* 25 See **Leann** This is the same "humoral" idea as has come down to us in the word melancholia, *μελαγχολία* from *μέλας* black + *χωλή bile*—Note, Col 25

Dúinte is from **dúin** *shut, close up,* the old idea of "**strictum**" as against "**laxum,**" the idea being that certain foods caused a closing up of the bodily "pores" and so brought about an unhealthy state, **dúinte isna taobhaibh** *constriction in the sides* 14, **am biadh améid andlistinaigh do ní dúinte** *food in unreasonable quantity will cause constriction* 4

Dúracht *desire*, **no aní eili bhus duracht lis** *or any other thing which he desires*—to say 9

Dusacht *awake-ness* **donit daoine imdha lá don oidchi ag codladh sa ló ocus in an dusacht san oidchi ocus is ro-olc sin** *many men make day of night, sleeping in the day and awake* (in their awakeness) *in the night—and that is very bad* 13.

E

Ealaidh *skill, art, science* **teagaisgidh an ealadha leighis "medicina docet"** *the means of cure teaches* 14—that is, a good inference as to the cause may be drawn from what cures the disease—quite correct, **glantur an t'aer go**

h'ealadhanach *the air is cleansed scientifically* "**secundum artem**" 27.

Eanbruithi, G **eanaraich,** *soup, broth.* This word has been a trouble to me for many a long day, and it has been a trouble to others The form **én bruith,** which is so common in the older language, has always led me to think that there was a *bird* **én** in it, philologically at any rate The late Dr Macbain thought it was from **in + bruithe** "in-boiled" *Cormack's Glossary* and O'Clery would make it from **én** *water* + **bruithe** *boiled,* and the late Whitley Stokes under the word **enghlas** *grey water* or thin gruel or *milk and water,* would point the same way. In this text it always means *soup* or *broth,* **gidhedh foghnuidh eanbruithi na písi** *nevertheless the soup of pease will suffice* 23

Édagh, G. **Aodach** *clothes, cloth,* **ocus cluthur le h'édach gomaith e** *and let him be well covered with clothes* 13

Edluis, "raritas" 15. I cannot give an English equivalent

Egla, G. **eagal** *fear,* **is éu-gal = ex-gal,** *wanting* or *void of valour* or *courage,* **ar egla na fellsamh ele** *for fear of the other philosophers* 28 The concept of manliness and courage in the Gaelic language is indeed very interesting The positive element is the right and natural factor in character always. The defect is always "**non**" or "**ex**" It was never there, or it has disappeared.

Égmais, G **eugmhais, as eugmhais** *without.* The word essentially means *want, defect,* and Dr Macbain is perhaps not very far wrong when he suggests that the word is **eu + comas** "non-power" which is really *want* and *defect* **Teid an dimaoinus gach ní dibh so an égmais an misuir** *all of these things will go into foolishness without the temperance* or *abstemiousness* 26

Égnaidh Adj from **éagna** *wisdom*. **dlighi in duine égnaidhi a caomhna fein ar fhín** *it becomes the wise man to spare himself of wine* 6, "**sapiens debet sibi prohibere vinum bibat**"

Eignighim *I force, compel* The stem is **éigin** *need, necessity* W **angen, na do meadon eignighadh** "**nec cogere uentrem**" *nor to force your middle, i e* belly 15, **na h'éignigh goláidir do shuigi** *do not forcefully compel thy seat,* that is, thy bowel—do not force it 6, "**nec cogas fortiter anum**" 26 **o aon gnodugh éigentach eile**

from one another (any) *necessary cause* 16, **égintus innfhuartha in croidi,** *the necessity for the coolness of the heart* 4

Eile, eili and **ele** *other, another,* W **aill,** Bret **eil,** Lat **alius,** Gk ἄλλος, Old Gaulish **allo**—as in Cæsar's *Allobrogi*, **naid leanda ele** *than other fluids* 20, **na nech eile** *than another person* 20, **do biadhuibh eile** *of other foods* 20, **ocus ataid fersadha eili ar an fíon** *and there are other verses upon the wine* 26

Eireochas from **eirghim** *I rise*, G **eirichim,** Lat **ērigo,** Eng. *erect* **intán eireochas neach** *when a person rises*—in the morning 9, **oir eirighitt na dhetaighi inmholta** *for it will rise in undesirable fumes* 5—Note

Éis *footstep, trace, death* The essential meaning is not clear The word now only remains in composite forms as **daéis** *after* and **taréis** *after* also, but with different Preps **do** and **tar** = "trans," the latter having a feeling of motion in it

Én *a bird*, G. **eun,** W **etn, edn,** Br **ezn,** all from an old root **pet** *fly*, **na h'éin do niter do droch rósdadh** *the birds that are badly roasted* 24, **gaile an éin renaburthar struccio** *the stomach of the bird named Struthios* 2.

Én *one* mod **aon, baindi ocus iasg ar én bórd** *milk and fish upon the one* (same) *table* 12 **na gabhthur .. én ní diureticach** *take not* (any) *one diuretic thing* 12, **saor in gach én ní** *free in each one thing*—in every respect 17; **oir ni fuil én ní coimedus nech ar eslaintibh** *for there is not* (any) *one thing which* (fore) *sees a person against diseases* —better than blood-letting 21, **ar én cor** *for* (any) *one reason* 14, **na caithid ar én cor iad** *let them not for any reason use them* 23, **én raod** *any part*, lit *one thing* 23, **o aon gnodugh** *from one cause* 16 **an éinecht** *in one time* 10—for **én** and old **fecht** *time*, **ocus én uair amhain** *and one time only* 20, **ocus is don milsi oenda tuighter sin** *and it is of the united* (single, simple) *sweetness this is to be understood* 19, **ar énchuid** *at one meal* 10.

Eochair *a key*, G. **iuchair,** W **egoriad** "the opening thing" **eochair gach uile eolais** *the key of all knowledge*—Hippocrates 28

Eoin Baisti (Féil). um fhéil eoin baisti *about the feast of John Baptist*—Midsummer Day, June 24th

Eolas *knowledge*, **eochair gach uile eólais Ippocras** *the key of*

all knowledge Hippocrates 28, **ocus ro[f]urail eolus ocus aithi báis** *and he commanded* (sought out) *the knowledge and time of death* 28.

Errach *Spring*, G **earrach.** This word seems based upon the old Keltic concept of the year The **Céitein**, the month of *May*, has its best rendering as the **cét-ain** or "first-time" of the year The **earr-ach** would then naturally be the "tail-end" as we have it in **earr-ball** *the tail* or end member, **sa geimredh ocus san errach** *in the Winter and in the Spring* 15—see **errannaibh**

Errannaibh from **err** *a tail*, G **earr**—which we have in **earball** *tail-piece*, really from **air** *after the after-member*, **isi nan errannaibh is ferr no is millsi na h'éisg ocus na mná "pisces et mulieres sunt in caudis meliores uel dulciores"** 18, **is fuar in t'iasg in an err** *fish is cold in the tail* 18.

Esbhuigh *want, defect*, G **easbhaidh** from or akin to **ex + bi** "to be out of", **tre esbhuigh an indfhuara** *through the absence* (or want) *of the coolness* 4

Espartan *twilight* Simply the Lat. **Vespertana**, G **feasgar**; **roimh an teirt ocus an uair na h'espartan** *before sunrise* (rather *the third hour*) *and in the twilight* 16.

F

Fadhó is the Prep. **fa + dhó** = *twice*, **is ferr began do caithimh fadhó** *it is better to use a little twice* 4 **fadhó no fathrí san aimsir cetna** *twice or three times in the same period* 15

Faduighim *I make longer, prolong* from **fada** *long* **ocus aimsir d'faidiughadh** *and to prolong the time* 10

Fágbhail *leaving*, from **fág** *leave*, **intán bhes ag a fagbhail** *whilst it* (the food) *is leaving* 8

Faghtur from **faghaim** *I find, get* **muna faghtur glan gu nadurdha e** *if it is not found clean by nature* 27 **ni fhaghann on biadh remhar do beith an íchtar** *it cannot find* (a way) *because the fat food is at the bottom* 10 **ocus gan blas an bidh d'fhaghbhail** *and not to get the taste of the food* 5

Fáill *delay*, G **dàil**, **ocus na cuiredh a faill** *and do not put it into delay* 9

Faon *poor, feeble*, **is olc codladh faon** *a poor sleep is bad* 13.

Farligettur; cad farligettur *what has been "let,"* "quem amiserunt"

Fásaid, fás *grow*, **nach fhásaid na daoine ginacha** *that the greedy* or gluttonous *men will not grow* 4.

Fásgadh *wringing, squeezing*, **nach maith fásgadh eigneach do denamh** *nor* (is it) *good to make an imperative squeezing* 15, **arna mberbadh ocus arna fásgadh** *after being boiled and squeezed*—through cloth 23.

Fastaighter from **fastinghim** *I stop, stay, retain*, **na fastaíghter ar én cor iad** *and let them not be retained for any reason* 14.

Feaghadh *seeing, observing*—see **aithfeaghadh** *re-seeing, compensation* 3, 21

Fecht *a time*, **began dotabhairt an ein[fh]echt** *a little given at one time* 16, **ocus ni gabhdhaois biadha examhla an éinfheacht** *and do not take "exemplary" foods at one time*—**exsamhla** here seems to have an *excessive* or *exceptional* meaning This old word remains in G hidden in **fathast** *yet* and in **am feasda** *forever*, the one being **fo-fecht-sa** "**sub hoc tempus**" and the other **in-fecht-sa** "from this time forward", **oir in biadh caither an einfhecht a meid móir ni h'éidir a dileaghadh** *for the food taken in large quantity at one time cannot be digested* 4

Féchuin *to examine, see, try*, **dleghur aimsir na bliadhna do féchuin** *it is necessary to examine the season of the year* 15, **dlighear na neithisi d'fheuchain** *it is right to try* (or examine) *these things* 3

Fédfuighi from **feudfaighim** *I can, must, am permitted*, **ni(fh)éidir no ni h'urusa** *it is not necessary nor easy* 10, **ocus o nach fédurus** *since you dare not* 10, **ni feduit** *they must not* 25

Féil *a feast, festival*. **um féil stefain** *about* (at) *St. Stephen's feast*, Aug 2nd **um fhéil eoin baisti** *at the feast of John the Baptist* 21 Note, Col 22.

Féin *self*, added to Personal Prons and to Nouns to make them Emphatic, **do aforismorum féin** *of his own Aphorisms* 20.

Fellsamh *philosopher*, **ar egla na fellsamh ele d'aghail dirradais** *for fear of the other philosophers getting his testament or secret*, 28

Fén *a section of a book*; **sa dara fén don cét leabur** *in the second section of the first Book* 2, **sa treas fén dég** *in the thirteenth section* 11.

Féoil *flesh, flesh-meat*, **seachnadh cáisi intán sin ocus feóil** *avoid cheese in that time, and flesh-meat* 22, **ocus a gnáthughadh dh'feóil ocus do biadhuibh eile oilius comaith** *and* (habitually) *using of flesh-meat and of other foods which nourish well* 20.

Feradh *excrement*, **indarbur an fual ocus in feradh** *let the urine and the faeces be expelled* 14. **in feradh fadhó no fathrí san aimsir cétna** *and defecation twice or three times in the same period*, **gan claochlogh do beith ar in fual na ar in feradh** *without change being upon the urine or the excrement* 4.

Ferg *anger*, **creit gurub dimaoin duit ferg do denamh** *and believe that it is folly of thee to make anger*—to get angry 25.

Férr and **fearr** *better*, **is i is ferr isna h'annminnthibh** *it is it that is better in the animals* 19; **toradh is ferr na iad** *a fruit that is better than them* 19.

Fersa *a verse*, **fersaighteoir** *a versifier*, **et do cuir in fersaightheoir fersadha ar follamnughadh na slainti** *and the versifier has put* (made) *verses upon the regulation of health* 25, **adeir in fersaigtheoir** *the versifier says* 21, **et ataid fersadha eili ar an fín** *and there are other verses upon the wine* 26.

Fhiacla from **fiacail** *a tooth*, G. **fiacaill**; **aindhsein a fhiacla** *and then his teeth* 9.

Fiarfuighim *I ask*, **is uime sin fiarfuighim** *it is therefore I ask* 6.

Fígeadha *figs*, from English, **na rísinedha ocus na fígeadha** *the raisins and the figs* 18, **déis na fígeadh** *after the figs* 19.

Fín and **fíon** *wine*, G **fíon**, W., Corn, Bret **gwin**, Lat. **vinum**, Gk **(ϝ)οἶνος**, **dlighitt nis mó d'ól d'fhín** *more of wine should be drunk* 21.

Fineal *fennel*, **ocus do bharr fhineil** *and of the tops of fennel* 23

Fiond *white*, **lucht lenna fiond** *those of white* (or pale) *humors* 25.

Fírindecha *truthful*, **mar do chuala o daoinibh fírindecha** *as I have heard from truthful men* 12. **antan bis an**

t'ocarus fírınnech ann *ın the tıme when real* (truthful) *hunger ıs there* 16

Fis *knowledge* **dlighear a fhis fós** *and you should know also,* 21, 24

Fithett, G **fichead** *twenty,* W **ugeınt**, Corn **ugens**, Bret **ugent**, Lat **vigıntı**, ıt occurs several tımes at end of Col 20.

Fiuchach from **fiuchaım** *I boıl*, **croccan fiuchach a fiuchadh ın t'uısgı** **Croccan** G **crogan** ıs an earthen vessel The expressıon here seems to mean *a burnt earthen vessel ın whıch the water ıs boıled* 8

Flichadacht *wet-ness, moıst-ness,* from **fliuch** *wet* Lat **lıquıdus; ag dul a tesoıghect ocus a bflıchadacht** *goıng ınto heat and ın moıstness,* 16, **na neithi flıchada** *the moıst thıngs* 24, **oır ge flıchadhı na neithi róstuighi** *for though the roasted thıngs are moıster* 24

Fodhailter from **fodhaılım** *I dıvıde*, **gıdheadh is an dá rannuibh fhodhailter aımsır na blıadhna** *yet* (or nevertheless) *ıt ıs ın two portıons that the seasons of the year are dıvıded* 21

Foghmhar *Autumn* The name seems to be **fo + gamur** "**sub hıemem**" the *under-wınter*, **do beirıd toirrthi an foghmhair caoinedh dermaır duıt** *Autumn fruıt wıll gıve thee sore weepıng* 16

Fóghnuidh *ıt wıll suffice*, **ocus fóghnuidh an aghaıdh an rema fhuar** *and ıt wıll suffice agaınst the cold rheum* 26, **et ıs mór fhoghnus fothrugadh uısgı mılıs** *and greatly wıll suffice* (the) *bathıng ın sweet water* 14

Foirbheartas *help, assıstance*, **ocus do nı foirbheartas do na cáırdıbh** *and ıt wıll make assıstance to the frıends,* that ıs, to frıendshıp—the wıne 26

Foillsighim *I show, demonstrate*, **dlighear d'foıllsıughadh** *ıt ought to be shown* 12, **mur ıs follus** *as ıs evıdent* 19, **mar foıllsighes galen** *as G shows* 1

Fóiridh *ıt wıll relıeve*, from **fóırim** *I relıeve, succour, heal* **ocus fóırıdh tınneas ın cınd go h'áırıghı** *and ıt wıll relıeve the headache especıally* 27

Foirm *form, manner*, **doréır foirme ocus nı doréır céime** *accordıng to form and not to degree* 1

Foirmeallach *external*, **on tes foırımeallach** *from the external heat* **go téıd an tes a bfuırmıll** *that the heat goes external*

16, **cum foirimill an chuirp** *towards the external* (parts) *of the body* 7

Fola Gen of **fuil** *blood*, **ocus re lucht fola deirge** *and with those of red blood* 25, **ocus togairmidh in fuil místa** *and it will call forth the monthly blood*—the menses 28

Follain *healthy* for **fo + shlán** "under wholeness," an extremely fine expression, **ocus is amhlaidh is follaine iat** *and it is so that they are the more healthy* 22, **mad áil let beith fallain** *if you wish to be healthy* 25 From **slán** *whole* comes **sláinte** *health* which is, and means *wholeness*, and even *holiness* is but an extension of the idea into the higher aspects of life The Saviour is magnificently called **Slánuigher** the giver of *wholeness*—"**sanator,**" and not "**salvator**" as other languages have it To be **follain** G **fallain** is to be enveloped in health as with a garment **Eu-slán** and **eu-sláinte** is *ex-health, disease,* "broken" wholeness, in the truest and most real sense No science can ever over-pass the perfect life-wisdom in these old words The science which does not see, acknowledge, and accept this simple basic fact of human life is not science and we have no use for it

It is a most valuable instruction to observe that the Gaelic language, in a fuller degree than perhaps any other tongue, expresses the attributes of manliness, health and courage in the positive form, and the defect of these, always, in the "ex-" form as being "out of" the natural state or condition **Eu-slaint** is *disease*—"ex-health." **Eu-cáil** is disease also but in lesser sense it means *out of condition* So also **eu-dóchas** *out of* or beyond *hope*, **eu-coir** *out of* or *beyond* justice, and many other similar expressions

It may be mentioned that there is no word in Gaelic for a coward The people who grew this language did not know the coward at all, but when in later days they unfortunately discovered him they called him **gealtair** or *madman*. This peculiar defect in the language is not perhaps more interesting than the way in which it was made good.

Follamhnuighim *I rule, order, govern*, **ar follamhnughadh na sláinte** *concerning the regulation of health* 1, **lucht an droch fhollamhnuighi** *those of bad rule* or conduct 17, **a**

leabur follamhnaighti na slainti *in the book upon the regulation of the health* 17.

Folmaighe from **folmhaighim** *I empty*, **ocus folmaighe si ona ballaibh ainmidhi** *and it will empty* (or draw from) *the animal members* 27, **is e folmughadh na cuislide** *the emptying of the vein* 20

Fona *under the, under his*, **a cur fona cinn** *to put it under his head* 28.

For-lethon *very broad*, "hyper"-broad, *Et* **is riaghail for lethon condlighear an biadh lenus do na méruibh ... do shechna** *and it is a comprehensive rule that the food which sticks to the fingers should be avoided* 25—for it is tough

Fós *yet, still*, **dlighear a chongmail fós** *it is right to keep it still* 17, **tuilleadh fós** *moreover.*

Fosgladh *opening*, **ocus ro-fhurail an uaigh.. d'oslucadh** *and he commanded the grave to be opened* 28

Fostoghadh from **fostaighim** *I stop, stay, seize*, **gan fostogh[adh] ainndeonach** *without compulsory stopping*—of the breath 7, **na fastaighter ar én cor iad** *let them not for one* (any) *reason be restrained* 14

Fothrugadh *bathing*, from **fothraigim** *I bathe*, G **fathraig** *bathe*, **fothrugadh uisgi milis** *bathing in sweet water* 14.

Fual *urine*, **na conaim ar th'fual** *and do not hold* (or restrain) *thy urine* 26, **ar galardha fuail** *against diseases of the urine* 28, **gan claoghlogh do beith ar in fual** *without change being upon the urine* 4

Fuara Adj pl from **fuar** *cold* W. **oer**, Corn **oir**, **le neithibh fuara** *with cold things* 3, **chum fuarachta** *towards coldness* 3, **an aimsir ro-fuar na ro-the** *in a time* (which is) *very cold or very hot* 21

Fuighill Gen of **fuidheal** *a remnant* **arson fuighill an alluis** *because of the remains of sweat* 9, **fuighlech tochluighthi** *what remains of desire*, "**reliquie desiderii**" 4

Fuilighidh *bleeding*, from **fuil** blood, **an adharc maille fuilighidh,** *the horn for the purpose of bleeding* 27.

Fhuind Gen of **fonn** *soil, land*, or *region*, **is cóir ní éigin do tabhairt d'aire do leith na h'aosi ocus in fhuind** *for it is right to give something of attention on behalf of* (concerning) *the age and the soil or district* 15

Fulang *suffering*, **is ro-urasa lis na sen-daoinibh in treiginus d'fhulang** *it is very easy for the old persons* (lit *men*) *to bear*

the abstinence 25, **is ferr fuilingit lucht lenna duibh e** *those of black humors suffer it better* 25

Fundamint, Lat **fundamentum** *base, foundation*, **ocus gan fundamhint ro-mór do denamh** *and so as not to make too great a foundation* 8.—Note.

Furail *to order, command*, **ro-fhurail an uaigh . . . d'oslucadh** *he ordered the grave to be opened* 28.

Furtaighi from **furtaighim** *I relieve, comfort*, **oir furtaighi** (MS **furtachaighi**) **sin an dileaghadh** for that will assist the digestion 12, **a meid fhurtachaighus** *to the extent that* (the sleep) *helps*—digestion 12

G

Gabatur from **gabh** *take*, W. Inf. **gafael**, Corn **gavel**, G. **gabhail**; **mar gabatar iat** *as they were taken* 12, **ocus na gabhthur lictuairi ro-tesaigi** *and let not a very hot electuary be taken* 12.

Gach *each, every*, Corn. **pop**, Bret. **pep**, Lat **quisque**. These and other forms of the word are most interesting to the student of language, **gach ní dibh so** *every one* (thing) *of these* 26

Gaires from **gair** *call, name*, G **goir**; **is neithi fuara gaires dibh sin** *these are called cold things* 2, **acht gairit errach d'aimsir measurdha** *but temperate weather is called Spring* 22—that is the "mean" between cold and heat, **gairther "preseruatiuum" do "seruatiuum" uair and** *preseruatiuum is called seruatiuum sometimes* 1.

Galardha *diseases*, **galardha fuail** *urinary diseases* 27 The word seems to be based upon **gal** *weeping* or I E. **ghel** *pain.* In Gaelic it always has a heavier meaning than **tinneas** which is also *disease*, but based upon the old idea of "**strictum**" or *tension.*

Galen. Note, Col 1

Gan, G **gun** *without*, **gan claochlogh do beith ar in fual** *without change upon the urine* 4, **gan cuirrineacht** *without cramp* or spasm 5.

Gaothmaracht *flatulency*, **on gaothmuirecht** *from the flatulence* 14, **gan gaothmairecht** *without flatulence* 5.

Geala Adj. pl. of **geal** *white*, **do persillidh no do cennduibh geala losa** *of parsley and of white heads of leeks* 23.

Geinemuin *to generate, create,* from **genaim**, G. **gin** *beget*, W **geni** *to bear*, Bret. **ganet** *born*, Lat **gigno**, Gk. **γίγνομαι**, **do geinemuin fhola arís** *to generate* (restore) *his blood again* 21, **on ginter droch leann** *from which bad humor is generated* 7

Geimredh *Winter*, mod **geamhradh**, W **gaem**, Bret **goam**, Lat **hiems**, Gk **χειμών**, **biadh remur a meid móir sa gheimredh** *fat food in good quantity in the winter* 21

Gendaois error for **dhéntaois** from **dénaim** *I do*, **do gendaois dúinte** *it will cause constriction* 14. **do gentaoi on línadh** *which are done from the fullness* 21

Geuraigi from **geuraighim** *I sharpen*. **ocus geuraigi in t'indlecht** *and it will sharpen the intellect* 26.

Gidhegh *nevertheless*, variously written **gidhedh** 1, **gidhegh** 2, **gideadh** 25, G **gidheadh = ciod + eadh** *though yes* or **ge(dh)-eadh**, **gidhedh bit misur maille ris** *nevertheless let moderation be along with it* 26

Ginacha Adj pl *greedy, gluttonous* **adeir Auicina . nach fhásaid na daoine ginacha** *Avicenna says that the gluttonous men will not grow* 4

Glan *clean*, **fíon glan "vinum purum"** *pure wine* 26, **dam bia in gaili glan** *if the stomach is clean* 22

Gluasacht *motion, movement*. **ocus bis ar gluasacht hégin** *and they would be on some movement* 19, **arson in gluasachta** *because of their movement* or activity 18 **gluasacht mór** *big effort* 12

Gná Imper of **gnáthaighim** *I use* or *accustom myself*, **a ro-gnáthughadh** *its over-doing* 20

Gné *kind*, Lat **genus**, Gk **γένος**, **is comór ata gach gné dibh mar sin** *and greatly is every kind of them so* 18 **ataid trí gneithi** *there are three kinds* or divisions, upon the regulation of health 1.

Gnímaighitt from **gním** *an action* **o thota species gnímaighitt na baill** *from* **"tota species"** *the members act* Note, Col 2

Gnimuighend from **gniomhaighim** *I act, perform*, **ar in gnimuighend** *upon which they act* 25.

Gnodugh *affair, business, cause*, G **gnothach**, **ach a nech bis gan toirmisg o aon gnodugh éigentach eile** *except the person who is without prevention—forbidden—from any other compulsory cause* 16

Goirteochar from **goirtighim** *I hurt* and secondarily *I make sour*, **oir goirteochar iad** *for they shall be hurt* 17, **na h'ubla goirti** *the sour apples* 18.

Goléor *sufficient* for **go + léoir** *up to enough* This is the expression that has been "lifted" into English as *galore*, where it means not *enough* but far more than enough—abundance, excess

Gominic *often* 19, may be taken as a type of Adverbial form which occurs very often In the next line **gomór** *greatly*, is "another of the same" The **go** is G **gu** *to*, Lat. **ad** or rather **usque ad** "up to", **goláidir** *strongly, forcefully* or *violently* 26

Grema Gen of **greim** *a bit, a mouthful*, **taréis th'sluigti an grema** *after thou hast swallowed the mouthful* 8

Gur, gurub, gurup, gurob 6 are subjunctive forms which may be rendered *that.* The elements are old **co** now **gu** + the verbal **ro** + a fragment of the verb "to be" **co-ro-ba mar an abair gurub** *where he says that it is* 2. **gurup le neithibh fuara** *that it is with cold things* 2, **gurob taréis** *that it is after* 6

Gustrasda = a working formula for **go san tráth-sa** *until now, lately*, **adubhrumar don chail gustrasda** *I have just said regarding the appetite*—"de qualitate cibi jam dictum est" 5

H

Hali. Note, Col 1

I

Iad *they, them*, **follamhnaighter iad** *they shall be regulated* 2, **go truaillter uile iat** *that they are all corrupted* 10, **toradh is ferr na iad** (any) *fruit that is better than them* 19

Iarraidh **(ag)** *seeking*, Inf. of **iarraim** *I seek, ask*. **ag iarraidh slighеadh amach** *seeking a way out* 10—see **fiarfuighim**

Iasg *fish*, **baindi ocus iasg** *milk and fish* 12, **seachnadh . iasg sailthi** *shun salted fish*—at that time of blood-letting 22, **is millsi na h'éisg ocus na mná** *that is sweetest of fish and of women* 18.

Ibhter from **ibhim** *I drink*, W **iben** "bibimus" Corn **evaf,**

Bret. **eva**, Lat **bibo**, **do ní ibhter** *concerning the thing that is drunk* 9

Ichtar *bottom, lower part*, the opposite of **Uachtar** *q v*, **ocus ni fhaghann on biadh remhar an íchtar** *still the fat food being under*(neath) prevents the other food passing 10, **gach eslainti dambia is na ballaib ichturuca** *every disease which may be in the lower members* or parts 27

Ím *butter*, W **ymenyn**, Corn **amenen**, Lat **unguen-tum**, **an t'ím umorro caitir roimh na biadhuibh e** *the butter indeed it should be used before the meals* 23

Imarctech, "**Potus delativus,**" **deoch imairctech** Note, Col 8

Imchubidh *proper, best*, **is roim an mbiadh is imchubidh i** *it is before food it is most proper* 8, **dambia aimsir imcubidh aige** *if he has sufficient time* 9.

Imdaighi from **imdaighim** (based on **imdha** *q v*) *I multiply*, G. **ioma** and **iomadh** *many*, therefore *I make-many*, **imdaighi na brigha "uires multiplicat"** *it multiplies the strength* 26, **na biadha d'imdhughadh** *to multiply the meals* —or more frequent 10, **is ferr na h'uaire d'imdughadh na in caindigecht mór** *it is better to multiply* the times than (to take) *a great quantity* 4—it is better to take food often than in great quantity at one time, **acht na huaire d'imdughadh** *but to make the times more frequent* 8

Imdha *many*, G **iomadh**; **daoine imdha** *many men* 13, **piana imda** *many pains*—"**multos cruciatus**" 26

Imighi from **imigh** *go*, **oir imighi roim in ndileaghadh** *for it goes before the digestion* 7.

Imlan *whole*, is **im** intensive and **lán** *full* · *completely full, intact, altogether*, **na h'almoint ocus a caitimh imlan** *that the almonds should be used*, *i.e.* eaten, *whole* 23, **dilighter gohimli e** *it* (the food) *is wholly digested* 13

Imli *wholly*, an Adverbial form—see **Imlan**

Ímpir *Emperor*, Lat **Imperator**; **táinic in t'ímpir** *the Emperor came* 28

Impogh from **impoighim** *I turn, move, convert*, G **iompaich**, Inf **iompaidh**, **ocus dlighur** (MS is **dilighur**) **impog ar in taobh ele** *and it is necessary to turn on the other side* 13, **ocus impogh arís ar in taobh ndeas** *and to turn again on the right side* 13, **gaothmuirecht ag impogh suas** *flatulence moving upwards* 14.

Imsnimh *sorrow*, **cuir imsnimh trom dít** *put heavy sorrow off thee*—away from thee 25 The word occurs in Windisch's *Texte* Sc. M. 4, **in imshnim mór** *in great sorrow.*

Imurcracha *superfluities*, **imurcracha na sróna** *the superfluities of the nose* 9.

Inadh G. **ionad** *a place*, **mar adeirur san inadh cétna** *as is said in the same place* 1, **an cét inadh** *the first place* or position 27—the word is used in this Col. several times, **sea h'induibh** *six places* or positions 27

Incinn *the brain*, what is "in the head," εν-κεφαλον, from **in + ceann** *a head*, **geuraichi in incinn** *it will sharpen the brain* 26

Indarbadh mod. **ionarbaim** *I expel*, **indarbadh ainnsein imurcracha** *let the superfluities be then expelled* 9

Inde *the "inward" parts, the bowels*, **lagaid na h'inde línta** *and they weaken* or *relax the full* (or overcharged) *bowels*—"**et uiscera plena relaxata**" 26

Indfhuara is **ind** *to, against* + **fuar** *cold*, G **fionnar** for **fionnfhuar** *cool*—**feasgar fionnar** *a cool evening*, **tre esbhuigh an indfhuara** *through the absence of coolness* 4

Indladh from **inlaim** *I wash*, **ocus indladh a lamha** *and let him wash his hands* 9

Indmuis *wealth, treasure*, G **ionmhas**; **d'iaraigh indmuis** *to seek treasure* 28

Indtlechta *intellect* Gen **na leisgi indtlechta** *nor laziness of intellect* 5, **ocus geuraigi in t'indtlecht** *and it will sharpen the intellect* 26 This seems to be directly from Lat **intellectus.**

Indstruimint the Eng *instrument*, Lat **instrumentum** *means, tool*, etc, **on tes mar indstruimint** *from the warmth or heat as the means* 2

Indtu *in them*, **in tes disgaoiles indtu** *the heat set free in them* 25, **in seregra bis inntu** *the seregra which is in them* 27.

Induibh for **inaduibh** *places, positions* **sea h'induibh** *six positions* 27

Inmheadhonach *internal*, **uime sin anbfuinnighter go h'inme[dh]onach é** *it is therefore that he is weakened internally* 16

Inmholta *offensive*, "unpraiseable", **na dhetaighi inmholta** *in offensive fumes*—or eructations 5. The word **inmholta**

seems to be here used as the direct opposite of the sense in which it is commonly used—but see Note.

Innis *tell*, **ocus is uime sin innisis Galen** *and it is therefore Galen tells* 18

Inntaighter from **inntaigim** *I change, convert*, **inntaighter a fuil deirg e** *it is converted into red blood*, **indtaighter fuil derg aros**, "convertitur in rorem in poris" 11

Intabhurta "give-able," *allowable*, **na neithead is intabhurta** *the things which are allowable* 9.

Intán *in the time, whilst*, from **in + tán**; **intán caither in biadh** *in the time in which the food is used* 10 **intán sin** *in that time* 10, 21

Inte 27 is for **inté** *the he, the person*, **inté caithius cainel go minic** *the person who uses the cinnamon frequently* 27

Ither from **ithim** *I eat*, **ní ithter ocus ibhter** *the thing that is eaten and drunk* 9, **dlighitt began d'ól ocus d'ithi** (only) *a little should be drunk* and eaten 21

Itir *between*, G **eadar**, W **ithr**, Corn **yntr**, Bret **entre**, Lat **inter**; **itir in dá slinnen** *between the two blade-bones* 27, **itir na h'áirnibh** *between the kidneys* 28

L

Lá *a day* **oir is e sin an lá nadurra** *for that is the natural day* 15.

Lachtach *loose* **dambia in medon lachtach** *if the middle* (the inside) *is lax* 18

Lactuca *lettuce*, **do lactuca ocus do bharr fhineil** *of lettuce and of the tops of fennel* 23

Láidir *strong*, **na h'éigingh goláidir do shuigi**, "**nec cogas fortiter anum**" *and do not compel too strongly thy sitting* = anus 26

Lagaidh from **lagaighim** *I weaken, relax*. **ocus lagaid na h'inde línta** *and it will relax the* (too) *full bowels* 26, **gidhedh lagaid na h'ubla rosdaighthi** *nevertheless the roasted apples will relax* 18

Lámhuibh Dat pl of **lámh** *a hand*, **ocus folmaighe si ann sin ona lamhuibh** *and it will there empty* (withdraw from) *the hands* 27

Lán *full*, W **llawn, laun**, Corn **len**, Bret **leun**, Lat **(p)lenus**, **ocus a meadhon lán** *and the middle* (stomach) *full* 19

Lár *the floor, the ground,* Lat. **planus**, Eng. *plain*, "the flat part", **ar lár na sliastadh** *on the flat part of the thigh* 27.

Leabhur *a book*, W **llyfr**, Lat. **liber**, **seathadh leabhur** *sixth book* 11, **leabhraibh eigin** *some books* 11

Leaghtur from **leagh** *melt*, **gurub ullma leaghtur** *that more readily is melted* 2

Leag *read*, G. **leugh**, Lat. **lego**; **do leag an cairt** *he read the deed* 28.

Leag *a gem, precious stone*, **no leag no seod mbuada** or *gems or precious jewellery* 28.

Leanna the "humors"—the old concepts of the *fluids* of the body, **lucht lenna fiond** *those of white* or pale *humors* 25, **lucht lenna ruaidh** *those of red humors*, **lucht na lenna duibh** *those of the black humors* 25; **do truailledh na lendann** *to corrupt the humors* 27 Note, Col 3.

Leasrach *the loins*, the base is **leas** *thigh* or *hip*, perhaps akin to **leth-as** *a side*. "**Deasaich do chlaidheamh air do leis**" *gird thy sword upon thy thigh* (Psalm 45, 3)

Leigheas *a cure*, same base as **liagh**, G **leigh** *a healer*, **na deocha leighis** *the curing or healing drinks* 8, **is dlighi leighis sin** *that is the necessary treatment* 7, **leighes** *medicine* 12.

Leis-féin *by himself, alone*, leis is the compounded pron prep masc. *with him* + **féin** *self* = *alone*, so **leis-fein** *with himself, alone* 28, **aní bhus duracht lis** *the thing which he desires* 9

Leisgi *laziness, slowness, slothfulness*, **na leisgi indtlechta** *or slowness of mind* or *intellect* 5.

Leitreachuibh Dat. pl of **leitir** *a letter*, **o leitreachuibh cindti** *from certain* (or reliable) *letters* 9

Lenus from **lean** *follow, adhere to, cling to*, **an biadh lenus do na méruibh** *the food which adheres to the fingers* 25.

Leór *enough, sufficient*, **is leór ansacht le lucht lenna fiond** *it is sufficiently heavy or those of white or pale humors—to bear abstinence* 25, **et is lór so** *and this is sufficient* 27, **is comurtha go caithind neach goleór** *it is a sign that one has eaten enough* 4. This is the phrase **gu leoir** that has come into English as *galore* plenty, abundance, which really means "up to enough"

Leth *half, side*, W. **lled**, Bret **let**, Lat. **latus**; **na neithi leat omha** *the things half-raw* 24

Lethon *broad*, G **leathan**, W **litan**, **llydan**, **ledan**, Gk. **πλατύς**, see **For-lethon**

Liagh *a physician*, G **lighiche; oir is ní fuar gairter on liaigh do nithe íseal** *for it is a cold thing that the physician calls low things*, **oir in teas íseal is fuar am bél in lega** *for the low heat is "cold" in the mouth of the physician* 2, **ocus ni mar sin do na leghuibh** *and not so of* (according to) *the physicians* 22

Lictuairi the old spelling of *electuary*, **na gabhthur lictuairi ro-tesaigi** *do not let a too-hot electuary be taken* 12

Linadar from lionaim—see **Línta**, *I fill* **an drong adeir gur línadar iad féin do biadh go minic** *those who say that they fill themselves with food often*—and that no harm comes to them 17, **is usa línadh na dighe na línadh an bidh** *for the filling* (satisfying) *with drink is easier than the filling with food* 22.

Línta from **líonaim** *I fill*, **na h'inde línta** *the filled bowels* 26 —in a constipated or gross condition

Lochran *a lamp*, Lat **lucerna**, akin **λευκός** *white*, **bidh mar lochrand bis ullamh cum baithi** *it is as a lamp which is ready to drown*—to go out 6

Loighett *diminution, reduction*—the irregular Third Compar of **beag** *small*, really a Noun, **na loighett and san anail** *or diminution in the breath* 4

Longadh is used for *supper*, but here most likely for *eating* generally, so **ar cét longadh** is *upon first eating*—or the first meal 6

Losa *leeks, porrum* **do cenndubh geala losa** *of white heads of leeks* 23

Losgadh *burning, singeing* **oir truaillett in biadh aga losgadh** *for the food is polluted, being burned* 12, **loisgfidhe on tes teinntighe e** *it will be burnt because of the fiery heat* 16

Luath *quick, swift*, **do niter an codladh go ro-luath** *sleep is made too quickly* 14, **dílligher go luath e** *it is quickly digested* 10

Luathrigh Gen of **luaithreach** *ashes, dust* **arson fuighill an alluis ocus in luaithrigh** *for the remnants of sweat and of dust* 9—which are on the skin G **luath** means *ashes*, W **lludw**, Bret **ludu**, Corn **lusu**

Lubra *leprosy, infirmity*, **ullmuighit nech cum lubra** *they predispose a person towards disease* 12

Luigha *less*, G **lugha**, W. **llai**, Bret **lei**, akin Lat. **levis**, and Sansk. **laghas** *light*, **oir is luigha an tes disgaoiles indtu** *for the heat is less that is set free* (is untied) *in them* 23, **uair eile ni luigha** *another time less*—shorter 22. See **Loighett** for Third Compar.—this is the First

M

Macaoim, **mac** *a son*, W **map**, **mab**, Corn **mab**, Bret **mab**, **Ogham maqoi**; **na daoine óga ocus aindsein na macoim** *the young men and then the sons* 25, **na machtaoimh** *the sons*—children 24 The word may be taken to mean "youths" or young people of both sexes as **sendaoinibh** "old men" means old people

Macoll, **macall** (B M 15403), W **mabcall**, *common avens*, **Geum Urbanum** For a good many old plant-names see *C.M.J*, April 1910

Madh, **mad** *if*, **mad do gnathuich nech** *if a person has practised—blood-letting* 20, **madháil let bheith édrum** *if you wish to be light* 14, **mad áil let beith fallain** *if you wish to be healthy* 25

Maidin *morning*, Lat **matutina**, Eng *matin*, **sa maidin** *in the morning* 9, **feoil amháin do caithimh sa maidin** *to eat flesh meat alone in the morning* 10

Maille *with, along with, for* **imb-an-leth** "by the side of" (Mb), **bit misur maille ris** *let moderation be along with it* 26.

Mairidh from **mair** *last, live* **ocus mairidh sin uair and ré mí** *and that will sometimes last through a month* 22

Maith *good*, W **mad**, Corn **mas**, Bret **mat**, **ni maith is na haeibh in ní is milis is in bél** *it is not good in the livers the thing that is sweet in the mouth* 19

Maotha *soft, smooth, mild*, Lat **mitis**, **na neithi maotha no boga** *the mild or soft things* 24, **toghtar in cuid is maeithi** *let the softer portion be chosen* 19

Mar, **mar sin**, **mar so** *so, like that, like this*, **ocus ni mar sin do na leghuibh** *and not so of the physicians* 22 **Mar** for **mod far** *where*, **mar an abair** *where he says* 5, 6

Márach *tomorrow*, G. **a maireach**, **arna mhárach** *on the morrow* 11.

Maratrum, Gk. μάραθρον, fennel Ovid **do maratrum ocus d'anis** *of fennel and anise* 12

Marcuidhecht *riding*, based on **marc** *a horse*, *horsemanship*, W Corn Bret **march**, **do siubul no do marchuideacht** *of travel or of riding*—not good, after meals 12

Maseadh = ma-is-eadh *if it is "yes," if so be it*, **maseadh toghtar in cuidh is maeithi** *nevertheless let the softer part be chosen* 19 It is **madegh** 17, **ocus madegh dligheàr a treigen go mall** *and if it be so, it should be given up slowly* or gradually

Meadhon *the middle*, W **mewn** *within*, Bret **y meton** *amidst*, Lat. **medianum**, **medius**, Gk μέσος It is used, perhaps euphemistically, for the belly—**na do meadhon d'éigniughadh "nec cogere uentrem"** 15, **ocus a meadhon lán** *and the belly-full* 19

Meas *estimate, judgment*, base of **measurdha** etc, which see, **doréir mhesa bis fogus don fhirindi** *according to the estimate that is near to the truth* 9 **measruighter aicidighi na h'anma** *let the diseases of the mind be considered* (measured) 13.

Measa *worse*, irreg Compar of **dona** *bad*, G **miosa**; **ni fuil ní is measa** *there is nothing that is worse* 10

Measardha *temperate, moderate*, "measured", **don corp measardha** *to the temperate body* 1 **o measurdhact** *from temperance*—abstinence 1

Mediana *the median or middle vein of the forearm* It runs into the median-Basilic and the median Cephalic at the bend of the elbow, **is i mediana dligher do ligen** *it is the median vein that should be opened* 20.

Médughadh from **méduighim** *I enlarge, increase* **an puls do médughadh** *to enlarge the pulse* 4 **an caindighect contínoidech do medughadh** *to multiply or increase the ordinary quantity* 8 **uime sin méduighter e** *therefore it is increased* 13 at 10 the word has a "side" but very neat meaning, **an biadh do meadughadh ris in ghaili** *to make the food the same size (quantity) as the stomach*—can bear or requires—*to equate it*

Megathegni lit. *his Great Work* **sa naoimheadh leabhur do megathegni** 20 Note, Haly Col 1

Méid *quantity, size, "measure,"* W **maint**, Corn **myns**, Bret **ment**, Lat **mensus**; **biadh remur a méid moir** *fat food*

in great quantity—in abundant measure 15—the base of **Médughadh**, which see

Meisg *drunkenness* G **misg; mar bis ag lucht na meisgi** *as will be to those of drunkenness* 5, **adeir drong gurub maith bheith ar meisgi uair sa mí** *some say that it is good to be drunk once a month* 5.

Méith *soft, sappy, juicy* the same word as **maoth** *q v.* but with a shade of difference in the later meaning, **na neithi ro-méithi** *the very soft things* 25

Menmuinn *mind*, G **meanmhuin** *mind, joy, gladness* and **meanmna** from **mén** *mind*, **gan truime do beith ar an menmuinn** *without heaviness being on the mind*, or spirits 14, **bith menma t'shuilbir agat** *have a cheerful mind* 13

Mér *a finger*, G. **meur, an meur tanuisti** *the second finger* 9, **an biadh lenus do na méruibh** *the food that sticks to the fingers* 25

Mercurial, *dog's mercury*, Mercurialis of the Euphorbiaceae **do sail-cuach ocus do mercurial** *of violet and of mercurial* 23

Mí *a month*, G **míos**, W. Corn Bret **mís**, Lat **mensis**, Gk μήν, Sansk. **más**, *a moon-th*, **uair sa mí** *a time* (once) *a month* 5.

Mian, G **miann** *desire, choice*, **is mian liumsa "placet mihi"** *I like* a short walk after a meal 12

Milis *sweet, tasty*, **in ní is milis isin bél** *the thing which is more tasty in the mouth* 19 The base is **mil** *honey—the* sweet thing, **uisgi na meala** *the water of honey* 5

Minic *often*, W. **mynych**, Corn **menough; dlighitt beagan do caithimh go minic** *a little should be used often* 24, **co cúisighind ro-minc aphoplexia** *that it will cause* (bring about) *apoplexy* 20, **an drong adeir gur línadar iad fein go minic** *those who say that they fill themselves often*—with food, let them take care 17.

Minica the Compar of **minic** *q v oftener*, **dlighitt . . cuisli doleigen nis minica** *it is necessary to let blood more often* 20

Misur *measure, moderation, reasonableness*, "in measure", **oir téid an dimaoinus gach ní dibh so an égmais an misuir** *for all things of these go into vanity* (are in vain) *without moderation* 26

Mó *greater*, W. **mwy**, Corn **moy**, Bret **mui**, Lat **major**, **in cuid is mó bis ar gluasacht** *the portion which is in greater*

motion 19. This is a very good instance of the impossibility of getting the Gaelic idiom into English, **in cuid is mó**, standing alone, means *the part that is greater* but here **mó** refers to the verbal **gluasacht** ·. *which is more greatly in motion.*

Modh *manner, habit, custom, reasonableness*, W. **modd**, Lat **modus**, **is olc an codladh ocus in nemh-codladh téid tar modh amach** *bad is the sleep and the non-sleep* (insomnia) *which goes beyond* ("without") *all reasonableness* 12

Moille *slowness* the noun from **mall** *slow*, **moille tuirlingha** *the slowness of descent* 11, **moille oiprighthi** *the slowness of the working*—of the digestion 11.

Moran *much*, from **mór** *great*, **ocus gan móran d'ól** *and without drinking much* 8.

Morgadh *corruption*, **ocus is cúis sin don mhorgadh** *and that is cause of the corruption* 4, **do lenduibh morguighthi** *of corrupt humors* 10, **do ni gach uile torradh . morgtha** *every ..fruit will make corruption* 18

Mothughudh, mothaighim *I feel, perceive*, **gan anmfainne do mothughudh** *without feeling weakness* 5.

Muin *back* or more often *top* The idiom it forms is peculiar. **Thig air mo mhuin** is *come on my back.* **Tha e air mo mhuin** is equally correct for *he is on my back* or *he is on top of me*—even if I am on my back **Air muin an eich** *on the back of the horse* **Biadh omh ar muin bidh leth-bruithi** *raw food on the top of half-cooked food* 11

Muinel *the neck* or perhaps better here *the chest*, **sínedh a muinel** *let him stretch his chest* 9

Muire Mary, *the Virgin*, **a trátha muire** *his Hail Mary* 9.

Muna G **mur.** The Irish form is from **ma** *if* + **ni** *not* · *if not* The G form is a shortened **mar-ro mur-robh** *if* (he was) *not*, **muna bia an duine óg** *if the man is not young* 20.

N

Nádur *nature* is borrowed, **mar is tusga tochluighes nádur e** *as nature more readily desires it* 14

Nadurra *natural*, **is sin is codladh nadurra and in codladh nach sechnann in oidchi ocus nach toirmisind in lá** *that is natural sleep which avoids not the night nor prevents the day*, 13.

Neach *a person, anyone*, W. Corn. Bret. **neb, nep**, **go caithfid neach goléor** *that a person has eaten enough* 4

Neimnechtarda *feebleness*, **do lucht na neimhnechtarda** *to those suffering from weakness* 1.

Neithibh Dat. pl. of **ní** *a thing, a food*, **le neithibh fuara** *with cold things* 3

Nem-codlaidh insomnia, "un-sleep", **ocus gan nem-codlaidh do beith air** *and without sleeplessness being upon him* 5

Nertaighi *will strengthen*, base **nert** *strength*, G. **neart**, W **nerth**, Corn. **nerth**, Bret. **nerz**, same as in Gk. ἀνήρ *a man*, **nertaighi in gaili** *it will strengthen the stomach* 26.

Nesa mod. **neasa** *next*, **na rannuibh is nesa don t'samhradh ...is nesa don geimredh** *the divisions* (times or days) *that are nearest to the summer*.. (and) *are nearest to the winter* 17

Nescoidedh *boils, ulcers*, **nescoidedh inmedonach** *internal ulcers* The word was, at this time, not used with any pathological precision, **nescoidedh inmedonach** *internal boils* 20—Note.

Ní *a thing, anything*, **gach ní** *everything* 9, **ni fuil ní is measa** *there is not anything worse* 10, **in ní is fearr blas** *the thing of best taste* 19, **én-ní** 21.

Ní the verb to *do, cause*, **do ní tes an t'samraidh urchoid** *the heat of summer will do harm* 16, **do ní lagadh** *it will cause relaxation* 22, **donít daoine imdha la don oidchi**, *many men make day of night* 13, **ocus do ní inadh... basilica** *and it will do* (empty) *the region of the Basilic vein* 27, **ocus do ní comfhurtacht an disnía** *and it will cause comfort to the dyspnoea* 27

Ni a simple negative, **ni doréir ceime** *not according to step* or degree 1, **ni certaighter** *it shall not be corrected* 4, **ni h'imchubidh in fín** *the wine is not proper*—after food 7, **ni mar sin** *not so* 22

Nigheadh *let him wash*, from **nigh** *wash*, **nigheadh a shúili** *let him wash his eyes* 9

Nigním *inaction*, **nach gabann nigním ona cosmailiuis** *that none effect is taken* (received) *from the similars* 1

Nis for **ní + is** "**id quod**" used in Comparison, **oir dlighidh an céim beith nis isle** *for the step* (degree) *ought to be lower* 2, fully expressed 19, **oir is e in ní is fearr blas** *for it is the thing of better* (best) *taste*—that best nourishes

No *or*, **no do lucht na neimhnechtardha** *or to those of weakness* 1, **no go tuitinn an biadh** *until the food has fallen* 6.

Nodluig, G **Nollaig** *Christmas*, from Lat **natalicia** *the Nativity*, **ligter uair and um nodluig i** *it is "let" occasionally about Christmas* 21

Nua *new, young*, G. **nuadh**, W. **newydd**, Bret **neuez**, Lat. **novus**, Sansk **navya**, **intán is nua e** *when it is new*—moon 21

Nuimir *a number*, from Lat **numerus**, **nuimir éigin** *some number*—or figure 11

O

O, G **O** and **bho**, Lat **ab** *from* and *since*, **o sin a mach** *from henceforth* 27, **o measurdacht** *from moderation* 1, **o cuttromacht** *from equipoise*—from a rightly balanced state 2, **o nach bi** *since there will not be* 4.

Oband *sudden*, **ocus ni gohoband** 7, **ocus ni go h'obonn** *and not suddenly* 17.

Ocarus *hunger*, G **acarus**, **fulang ocaruis** *the feeling of hunger* 10, **an t'ocarus firinneach** *the truthful* (real) *hunger* 16.

Ocus *and*, G **agus**, W **ac** The word occurs very frequently It is the same base as in **fagus** *near*. **Agus** is close conjunction, **fagus** perhaps **fo + agus** is "under" or just short of **agus** *i.e near*

Oenda *single, simple*, **don milsi oenda** *of the single sweetness* 19.

Ofrit, **dofrit** bad writing for **do fuairit**, *they found*, **ocus is e ní dofrit and** *and what was presented there*—was a box 28

Óga pl of **óg** *young* The Welsh **ieuanc** and Bret **iaouank** are suspiciously like *young*—but they are all from the same origin, **na daoine óga** *the young men* 24, **munabia an duine óg** *if the man is not young* 20

Oi occurs frequently for **oir** *for qi*, **oi ni fuil an tes gearr and** *for the heat is not short in it* 15, **oi dan dernadh dia dighultus** *for if God made revenge* 17, **a cét oi = an cét uair** *the first time* 17. All this suggests a lisping defect of speech in the writer

Oidchi *night*, **is in oidchi** *in the night* 14, **super na h'oidhce** *the supper of night* 14, **san oidche** *in the night* 14.

Oileamhuin *nourish* from **oilim** *I rear*, **da tabhairt da**

oilemhaine *given to nourish it* 2; **dligher an drong so d'oileamhain le biadh leighiseamail** *for such should be nourished with healing food* 2, **ocus is uime sin nach oilenn se godlistinach** *and it is therefore that he is not nourished rightly* 4.

Oiprugh[adh] from **obairighim** *I work* The base is E Ir, **opair**, G. **obair** *a work, labour,* from Lat **opus**, **-eris** *a work* or *task*, **conach truaillter a oiprugh[adh]** *so that its operation shall not be corrupted* 26

Oir *for* is really the preposition **air** used as a conjunction The same occurs with **o** *from* which is used also as conjunction *since*, **oir is le biadh** *for it is with food* 2, **oir mar a duburt artús** *for as I said at first* 3

Oireat, G. **urad** *as much*, **oireat in méid is teo** *as much of the warmer portion* 10

Oisreaghdha pl. of **oisire**, G. **eisir** *an oyster*, **mar ataid na h'oisreaghdha** *as are* (or such as) *the oysters* 24.

Ól *drink*, **bit daoine ann lebáil móran d'ól** *there are men who would like to drink much* 21, **fín d'ól taréis bidh** *to drink wine after food*—is bad 6.

Olc *bad, evil* akin to Lat. **ulcus** *a wound* and Eng *ulcer*, Gk ἕλκος, **ata in gnathughadh coitcind ina aighidh so gu h'olc** *the common custom* (or practice) *is against this badly* 18

Omh *raw, unprepared,* G **amh**, W. **of**, **na neithi omha.. ocus na neithi leat omha** *the raw things and the things half raw* 24

Ona is **o** *from* + the pl Art—*from the* **truailleadh tic ona toirthibh** *the corruption which comes from the fruits* 18.

Opair *work*, G **obair**. **moille opairthi** *the slowness of working* 11—see **Oiprughadh.**

Órd is simply the Lat **ordo** *rule, order*. **d'órd in dieta no caithme in bídh** *of the regulation of diet or the* (proper) *use of food* 9

Orra *upon them*, **ocus cumdach orra** *and a covering* upon them 25. The Prep. pron. from **air** *upon* It is **uirri** 8, **ocus nach uirri** *and not upon it*, where it is Sing. fem to **coda**, **ocus bidh rabhaile orra** *and greediness will be upon them* 6

Ortomia miswritten for **ortonia** *Orthopnœa*, **ocus an asma ocus an ortomia** *and the asthma and the orthopnœa* 27 Gk ὀρθός + πνοή *breathing* (only) *upright*

Osluigthi *open*, mod **fosglaım** *I open*, **ocus in bél osluigthı** *and the mouth open* 13

Osoin amach *from henceforth*, lit **o sin a mach** *from that outwards* 27.

P

Paciencia, "*patience*" *monks' rhubarb*, **Rumex patientia**, **do spınarchıa ocus do paciencıa** *of spinache and of patience* 23

Partegul, Lat **partıcula**, dim of **pars** *a part*, **sa dara partegul** *in the second (p)article* 12.

Peaduir *St Peter*, **a féıl peaduır** *in Peter's feast* 22—June 29th

Pecadh *a sin, transgression*, ıs from Lat. **peccatum**, **in gach én pecadh** *in every one sin* 17

Péiredha *pears* from Eng., **mar ataid péredha** (such) *as are pears* 18

Persillidh *parsley*, **do saithsi ocus do persillidh** *of sage and of parsley* 23, **do bharr fhıneil ocus persillı** *of fennel-top and parsley* 23

Piana *pains*, **pıana imda** *many pains*, "**multos crucıatus.**" It ıs **poen** ın Welsh, Corn **peyn**, Bret **poan**, Lat. **poena**, Gk. **ποινή**, **is mór an pian do goıle super na h'oıdhce** *the supper of night is great pain to the stomach* 14—Note.

Pís *the pea*, **an pís umorro** *the pea however* 23, **pís úr** *new pease* 23.

Póir *a pore*, **a póirıbh ın gaile** *in the pores of the stomach* 12 **oır atá in croicınn póıremhaıl** *for the skin is porous* 9

Pónair *beans*, **pónair na pís** *beans or peas* 23—the sing forms are here used, ın the "collective" sense, for the plural.

Potaitsi *pottage*, **uaır imchubidh caıthme ın potaıtsı** *the proper time to use or take the pottage* 23

Proinnighthi the tıme *of eating* from **proinn** *dinner, a meal*, Lat **prandium** ın Old Irish **praınd**, **uair ın proinnıghthı** *the time of eating* 16, ıs **proındıughadh orduıghthı** *it is ordered, correct dietary*—to take food three tımes ın two days 11.

Ptısisi *phthısıs*, **lucht na ptisısi** *those of phthısıs*—phthısıcal people 23

Q

Quartana *quartan fever*, **a caibidil leighis in quartana** *in the chapter which treats of quartan* (fever) 10.

R

Rabhaile *foolishness*—or perhaps stronger. Irish has **rabhaidhil** for *raving*, but that seems too strong here Perhaps the *greediness* of old age would be very near the first intention, **ocus bidh rabhaile orra** *and they suffer from greediness* 6.

Radh the Inf. of irreg. verb **abair** *say*, **ocus tic lis an radh so Auicina** *and A comes with this saying* 11

Radharc, G. **fradharc** *sight, power of vision*, **is ro-mor urchoidighius in biadh san oidche don radharc** *the food taken at night greatly hurts the sight* 14

Ráithi *a quarter of a year*, **ré mí no ré ráithi** *during a month or during a quarter* 12.

Rann *a portion, division*, **indus go roindfigter in dá lá nádurra.. go comhtrom a trí rannuibh** *so that the two natural days* (48 hours) *are equally* (or better *evenly*) *divided into three* (equal) *portions* 11, **an dá rannuibh** *in two divisions* 21.

Rannchuidid, see **Rann**, **oi[r] rannchuidid ris in samhradh ocus reis an geimhredh** *for they are divided between the summer and* (against) *the winter* 17.

Ré *throughout*, "the space of", **ocus mairidh sin uair and ré mí** *and that lasts sometimes for a month* 22, **ré sea huairibh dég** *during sixteen hours* 12, **ré ocht n'uairibh dég** *during eighteen hours* 12

Ré *the moon*, **intán is airsuigh in ré** *when the moon is old* 21, **adeir do leith in ré mar so** *he says regarding the moon—as follows* 21

Recha d'ég *he will not go to his death* "cur morietur"

Reime *fatness*, G **reamhar** *fat*, W **rhef** *thick*, **o reimhe ocus oríghne** *from fatness and from toughness* 12

Rem-coimhett "**pre-seruatiuum**" *pre-serve*, **in corp dobáil do rem-choimett** *the body you would desire to preserve* 3,

preseruatiuum i. rem-coimed preservativum *that is fore-guarding* 1.

Rema fhuar *the cold rheum*, a borrowed Greek word, **ocus foghnuidh an aghaidh in rema fhuar** *and it will suffice against the cold rheum* 26 The Adjective is not in Agreement. It should be **an rema fhuair** The meaning of the expression is now not easy to understand

Remur *fat*, **tabhartur biadh remur sa gheimredh** *let fat food be given in the winter* 15, **na neithi remhra** *the fat things* 24.

Ria *to them*, Mod **riu**, **na daine dambia cudrumacht ria** *the men to whom is equableness*—ceteris paribus 19

Riaghail *a rule*, G **riaghailt**, Lat **regula**. **et is riaghail forlethon** *for it is a very broad* (comprehensive) *rule* 25, **riaghail do bir Damasenus** *a rule which D. gives* 20

Righinn *tough*, **ríghne** *toughness*, **o reimhe ocus o ríghne** *from fatness and from toughness* 12

Ríghthigh for **righe**, G **ruighe** *the forearm*—the base in **ruigheachd** *reaching*. **ar bunuibh in righthigh** *upon the roots* (proximal ends) *of the forearm* 27

Rísineadha *raisins*, **déis na fígeadh ocus na rísinedh** *after the figs and the raisins* 19.

Roime *before*, *before it*, **go fétfadh stuider do dhenamh déis bídh mar do dénadh roimhe** *that study may be made after meat as done before it* 5.

Rósdagh *roasting*, **na h'éin do níter do droch rósdadh** *the birds that are badly roasted* 24, **neithi róstaighti remra** *roasted fat things* 24, **na neithi rostuighthi** *the roasted things* 24

Ruadh *red*, G **ruadh** *ruddy*, W **rhudd**, Corn **rud**, Bret **ruz**, Lat **rufus**, Gk **ἐρυθρός**, **lucht lenna ruaidh** *those of ruddy humors* 18

Ruigim *I reach, attain to, experience*, **ypocondria do righeadh** *to experience hypocondria* 4, 5.

S

Sail-cuach *the violet*, **potaitsi do . ocus do sail-cuach** *a pottage of . . and of violets* 23. The Gaelic name is pretty and appropriate **sáil** *a heel* + **cuach** *a cup*, from the hollow spur formed by the lower of the five petals This is the same word **cuach** which has gone into lowland Scottish as **quaich** a drinking-cup.

Saithsi *sage* borrowed from English, **do saithsi ocus do persillidh** etc *of sage and of parsley* 23

Saland *salt*, **maille saland ocus re cuimin** *along with salt and with cumin* 23, **ocus iasg sailti** *and salted fish* 22

Salchur G. **salchar** *filth* from **salach** with root **sal** *to dirty*, **glantur salchur na súl** *the filth of the eyes is cleansed* 27.

Samhradh *summer*, **sa t'samradh** *in the summer* 23, **ocus isin th'samradh** *and in the summer* 13, **eslaintibh in t'samhruigh** *the diseases of the summer* 21.

Saothair, *labour, exercise*, **a h'áithle sin denadh saothair ocus siubhal mesarrdha** *after that let him do exercise or moderate walking* 9, **déis in thsaothair** *after the exercise* 9.

Sástur from **sásaim** and **sásaighim** *I satiate, satisfy*, G **sáth** *plenty*, Lat. **satis**, **gurub amlaidhi shásfaidhter in corp** "**sic corpus reflce**" 14, **oir sástur in nádur o began** *for nature is satisfied from a little* 14

Sáth *satiety, plenty*, base of **sastur** etc. which see, **ni dligheann neach a sháth do caithimh** *a person should not eat his "fill"* 10.

Scruball, Lat **scrupulus**, the twenty-fourth part of an ounce 28 —twenty grains

Sea *six*, **seathadh** *sixth*, **sa caibidil deighinuigh don seathadh leabhur do Colliget** *in the last chapter of the sixth book of Colliget* 11; **sea huair dég** *sixteen hours* lit. *six hours* (and) *ten* 11.

Seachnadh from **seachainim** *I shun, avoid, miss, pass by*, **seachnadh cáisi** *avoid cheese* 22, **dlighear an biadh righin do shechna** *the tough food should be avoided* 25

Seachran *an error, going astray*, **adeirit drong go seachranach** *some erroneously say*—that etc 2, **ocus seachranuighi brigh dileaghaidh an gaili** *and it will pervert the power of digestion of the stomach* 4, **is coithcenn t'shechranuighius in drong lerbáil cuisli doligen um féil stefain** *those commonly err who would wish to bloodlet about the feast of Stephen* 21, **madho rindeadh sechran** *if an error* (or mistake) *was made* 11, **ocus is sechranach do níd sin** *for they are wrong who do this* 17, **condentur sechran mór** *that a great mistake is made* 21

Secired *secrets*, **secired a chroidi** *the secret of his heart* 28 The *heart* is sketched, not written

Sefalica written for **Cephalica** *q v*, 27, the outer superficial vein of the upper arm

Seiledh *mucus*, G **seile** *spittle, rheum.* **Glas-sheile** is G *water-brash* The meaning here 9 is to cleanse the nose and chest, **indarbadh ainnsein.. le seiledh ocus le himur-cracha na sróna** *let these things be expelled with the mucus and the superfluities of the nose and chest* 9

Seimh *mild, placid, tender*—used in the text of things more easily digested, **oir is seimhe in chilus na in t'aran** *for the chyle is tenderer* (nearer digestion) *than the bread* 11.

Sen *old, aged*, **na sen-daoine** *the aged men*, **mar na sen-daoinibh** *like the old men*—or persons 24, **na sen-daoine on t'sendacht** *the old men from their agedness* 25, **an sen-duine on thsenordhacht** *the old men from their great agedness* 6. **Senordhacht** has a specific meaning = the fifth age of life "from 54 to 84" O R—Note, Col. 6.

Seregra *dry eczema?* Lat **seresco**, **ocus fóiridh in seregra bis inntu** *and it will relieve the seregra that is in them* 27.

Sesamh *standing* from **seas** *stand*, Lat **sisto**, Gr ἵστημι; **oir is ferr cumsanadh ina sesamh** *for it is better to rest standing* —or not in motion 12.

Sesar, *Caesar*, **tainic in t'impir .i. Sesar** *came the emperor that is Caesar* 28

Sgairt *the diaphragm* the "separator" from **sgar** *separate*, **ar in sgairt** *upon the diaphragm* 4.

Sgeigheadur for and from **sgeathaim** *I vomit, reject*, **gur sgeigheadur bídh ocus leighes . mar gabatar iat mí roime sin** *that food and medicines were vomited just as they were when taken a month before that* 12

Sgríbhadh *writing, to write*, **do[s]gríbadh** *to write* 28, **oir is doigh gurub e in sgribneoir fuair nuimir éigin sgribhtha** *for it is most likely that it was the writer* (copyist) *who found some number written*—and mistook it, placing *nine* by error for *sixteen* 11

Siasanach *a humming, singing noise*, **oir do gendaois. siasanach isna cluasaibh**, *for they cause a singing in the ears* 14

Simphoreanuis 22 **ocus in fhoghmar a féil S** *and in the autumn in the feast of Simphoreanus*—Aug 22nd.

Singcoipis Gk. συγκοπή *a fainting away, swooning*, **isin t'singcoipis tig o anmhfainne** *in the syncope which comes of weakness* 7.

Sínedh 9 and **sínfedh** 12, from **sínim** *I stretch*, **sínedh artús a lámha** *let him stretch at first* (or first thing) *his hands—arms* 9, **ri sínfedh sin** *with the stretching* (or extending) *of that* 12, **ni do réir shínte na cainndighechta** *and not according to the extension of the quantity* 15

Sínnsir *ginger*, **dlighear a caithimh maille sinnsir** *it ought to be used along with ginger* 18

Sír, G. **sior** *long, continual, constant*, W Corn Bret **hír**—the base of **síorruidh** *ever-lasting* and **gu siorruidh** *forever*, **abair gurab fallain na cnó do sír do na h'aeibh** *say that the nuts are always healthy for the livers* 19. I think the scribe, as myself certainly, was nearly misled by the contiguity of **Abhfullana** *nuts for* "**gur abfallain**" here, for the writing clearly shows the correction

Sirioipighi *the syrups*, **mar ataid na siriopighi** *as are the syrups* 8.

Siubhal *motion, a movement, journey*, **an biadh aga chur ar siubhal** *putting the food in motion* that is causing diarrhœa. The word is in common use for diarrhœa, **tha siubhal air** *he is relaxed* It is also used for *death* in a high and fine sense, **shiubhail e** means *he is dead*, but literally *he is gone*—on a journey. Gaelic has no expressed concept of the individual extinction by death. **Chaochail e** is perhaps the most common expression in everyday use and it simply means *he has changed* the same as is used for a change in the weather or in the face of the sky. **Siubhal áilginach** *a gentle walk* 12, **siubhal mesarrdha** *a moderate walking* 9.

Sláinte is simply *wholeness* based upon **slán**

Slán *whole, healthy* Lat **salvus** *safe* and **solidus** *firm* and the Gk. ὅλος = σολϜος *whole* are all akin in origin and idea as in form —See **Slainte** and **Euslaint**.

Sliastadh Gen of **sliasaid** *the thigh*, **ar lár na sliastadh** *upon the floor* (or flat part) *of the thigh* 27

Sligheadh *a journey, a way*, G. **slighe**, **ag iarraidh sligheadh amach** *seeking a way out* 10

Slinnen *the shoulder-blade, scapula*; **itir in dá slinnen** *between the two shoulder-blades* 27

Slug *swallow*, **taréis thsluigti an grema** *after the swallowing of the mouthful or bite* 8.

Snamh *swim* Lat **no, navi**, Gr ναώ, **no do beradh ar snamh e** *or it will be set swimming*—the food 8, **am biadh ar snamh sa ghaili** *the food a-swim in the stomach* 5.

Socamhuil *rest, ease*—same base as in G **socair** *ease* and in **sochd** *silence*, **ataid naoi socamhuil do beir in fíon glan duit** *there are nine eases* (rests, pleasures) *that clean* (pure) *wine gives thee* 25.

Sofena *the Saphenous vein*—in this case almost certainly the external or short Saphenous, because the operation is **ar lár na colpaid** *on the floor* or *flat of the calf*, where the Ext. Saphenous runs 28.

Soithech *a vessel, dish*, **gidhedh da faghaid in soithtech nemh-glan truaillter gu ro-urusa iad** *nevertheless if the vessel is got unclean they are easily polluted* 22.

Spinarchia, *spinache*, **ocus do spinarchia** *and of spinache* 23—garden spinache, **spinacia oleratea.**

Spirutalta *spiritual*, **folmaighe si ann sin ona ballaibh spirutalta** *it will then* (or perhaps better *there*) empty (or draw away) *from the spiritual members* or what would now be called "the higher centres"—compare **na ballaibh ainmhidhi** *the animal parts* 27.

Squinancia, Old Eng *Squinancy, Quinancy, Squinsy, Quinsy* Gk. κυνάγχη; **ar egla squinancia** *for fear of quinsy* 20.

Srón *the nose*, **imurcracha na sróna** *the superfluities of the nose* 9.

Stefain (**Féil**) *the feast of St Stephen*, **um féil stefain** *about the feast of Stephen* 21.—December 26th

Stipeghdha from Lat **stipo** *I press closely together* · *constipating*, **dlighear torrtha stipeghda do chaithemh** *constipating fruits ought to be used* 18.

Stranguria στραγγουρία *a choking of the urine*, "**stranguria interpretatur guttatim urine emissio**" **ionnarbadh an fhuail na braonibh** 28.

Struccio, *the ostrich*, Lat **struthio**, Gk στρουθίων.

Stuider *study* seems to be just the Eng word borrowed It has a very un-Gaelic feeling.

Subhaltach *joyful* from **subha** *pleasure, delight*, G **subhach** *merry*, the opposite of **dubhach** *sad*—for **so-bo-io** and

do-bo-io "well be-ing" and "ill be-ing", **ocus do bir in croidhi subaltach** *and it gives the merry heart* 26

Substaint, the Lat. **substantia; na bit én raod da substaint and** *let there not be anything of its substance in it* 23

Suighi *the seat,* **"anus", na h'éigingh go láidir do shuighi "nec cogas fortiter anum"** 26. **Muna dernter angar do beith a suighi e** *if it* (sleep) *is not done in a nearly sitting position* 13.

Suilbhir *cheerful*, **bith menma t'shuilbir agut** *let you have a cheerful mind* 13.

Suili (na) *the eyes,* **súil** *an eye,* W **haul,** Corn **heuul,** Bret **heaul,** Lat **sol**—*the sun* The eye is the sun of the body as the centre of our planetary system is its great light, **eslainti na súl** *diseases of the eyes* 27.

Suiper the Eng *supper*, **ocus na denuid acht super beg** *and do not* (take) *but a small supper* 22

Sul *ere, until*, **sul do biritt dan [a]íri iad** *before they are brought to their attention* 24, **sul dileaghtar go h'imlan e** *before it is entirely digested* 11.

T

Tabhair *give*, **na neithead is intabhurta** *the things that are forbidden* "un-give-able" 9, **ni dlighear atabhairt déis na coda** *it should not be given after the meal* 6.

Tachmaingnid from **tachmaingim** *I surround, embrace*, **ocus gu tachmaingind e** *and that it is surrounded* 13

Tadhbais *firm, thick*, **línadh tadhbais o lenna ruadha** *a thick fullness from red humors* 10

Taidhillter from **taidhim** *I adhere, join to*, **intan taidhillter e** *in the time* (or when) *it adheres* 25

Taighter from **taig** *custom, habit*, **an aimsir as an dtaighter an indharbadh** *in the time in which it is customary to expel them*, that is, the usual personal habit 14.

Táinic *came*, "vēnit" **táinic in t'impir** *the emperor came* 28

Tairngter from **tairngim** *I pull*, **conach tairngter an biadh cum nan ae** *so that the food may not be drawn towards the livers* 13, **ar na tarruing cum béil an ghaili** *being drawn towards the mouth of the stomach* 10

Tanuisti anything *second* whence **tanist** *heir apparent*, **an meur tanuisti** *the second finger* 9, **Pilip tanaisi an tíre**

P the tanist or *heir-apparent to the government* O.D., **hi persin tanaisi "in persona secunda"** Sg

Taobhaibh, taobh *a side, flank* The Welsh, Corn and Bret is **tú** and the word is indeed so *pronounced* largely over the North of Scotland, **do gendaois duinte isna taobhaibh** *it will cause constriction in the sides* 14

Tar *over, across, beyond,* W **tra,** Lat **trans,** Sansk **tar, na neithi. connaimhter tar oidchi** *the things that are kept over night* 25, **ocarus tar a gnáthughadh** *hunger beyond ordinary*—beyond customary 10

Tarbhach *useful, profitable, effectual*, **caindighecht is tarbhach** *the quantity that is useful* 8 **is tarbhach cum an dileaghtha tart d'fhulang** *it is effective towards digestion to suffer thirst* 8

Tharr, do tharr in bradain *as regards the belly of the salmon* 19

Te *hot,* G **teth, gach uile ní inafuil betha is te e** *everything in which is life is warm* 3, **na cuirp theo** *the warm* (or hot) *bodies* 3, **arna theghadh** *after being warmed* 9

Teagaisgigh from **teagaisg** *teach, instruct*, **teagaisgigh an ealadha leighis** *the skill of healing teaches* **"medicina docet"** 14.

Teasargadh from **teasargaim** *I save, rescue*, **fettur a remh'-choimed no a tesargadh re neithibh fuara** *it may be prevented or saved by cold things* 2, **do teasargadh ar na h'eslaintibh** *to save against the diseases* 21.

Teghni, Gk τεχνῆς; **sa treas partegul do theighni** *in the third particle of his Work* 2

Téghmand, from **tégmais** *it happens*, **oir ni thegmhand so** *for this would not happen* 4

Teine *fire*, **na sa teine** *than in the fire* 2, **go gar do theine** *close to a fire* 22

Teintighe *fiery* based on **teth** *hot* and **teine** *fire,* W, Corn, Bret **tan do loisgfidhe on tes teinntighe e** *it would be burned because of the fiery heat* 16

Teirt *sunrise*, **roimh an teirt** *before sunrise* 16. Note, Col 13

Tes *heat, warmth,* W **tes,** Corn **tes,** Bret **tez,** Lat **tepeo,** Eng *tep-id*, **oir in teas íseal is fuar am bél an lega e** *for the low heat is "cold" in the mouth of the physician* 2, **le neithibh tesaighi** *with warm things* 3 **go fuil an fín tesaighi tirim** *that the wine is hot* (and) *dry* 3, **tre tes na h'aimsiri** *through* (because of) *the heat of the season* 21.

Texa *a text*, from English, **a coimint an texa so** *commenting upon this text* 2, **ag tuigsin an texa sin** *understanding that text* 2

Timprail not a very Gaelic word It means "stirring up", **arna coimusg ocus arna timprail** *mixed and stirred*—the food in process of digestion 8.

Tindsgaint and **Tinnsgnius** from **tinnsgnim** *I begin, commence*, **cend do tinnsgaint an geimhrigh** *the head of the beginning of the winter* 22, "**iemis caput est orientis**"; **go tabhair tindsgaint loighi . furtacht mór** *that the beginning of lying down*—an after-rest—gives great assistance to digestion 13, **cahuair thinnsgnuid aimsira na bliadhna** *what time the seasons of the year begin* 22.

Tinneas *sickness*, here *pain* **tinneas in cind** *pain of the head* = headache, retaining the old pathological idea of "**strictum**" or tension. It is widely used now, as here of *pain* **ocus fóiridh tinneas in cind goháirighi** 27, **tinneas na h'urchoid** *orchitis* **tinneas mara** *sea-sickness*, **tinneas cléibh** *chest disease*, etc

Tirim *dry*, **na cuirp tirma le neithibh tirma** *the dry bodies with dry things* 3, **le neithibh tesaighi tírma árda** *with warm, dry, high things* 3

Tirmuighi from **tírmuighim** *I dry*, **oir tirmuighi an stuidir iad** *for the study makes them dry* 24.

Tochlughadh *desire*, **intan tinnsgnius a thochlaghad go nádura** *when his desire* (for food) *begins naturally* 9, **na tuitim tochluighi do beith air** *nor that a failure of desire* (appetite) *should be upon him* 5, **fuighlech tochluighthi** *remnant of desire* "**reliquie desiderii**" 4.

Togairmigh *will call forth* from **to + gairm**, **togairmigh an t'allus** *it will call forth the sweat* 26, **togairmidh in fuil místa** *it will call forth the monthly blood* = menses 28

Toghtar from **toghaim** *I choose, select* **sa geimhredh toghtar in uair bhus teo** *in the winter the warmer time is chosen* 17. **uair toghnidhi na bliadhna** *the chosen time of the year* 21

Togra *inclination, desire, disposition* **arson na togra ata aige** *because of the inclination it has* 1

Toirmisges, from **toirmisgim** *I forbid, hinder, prevent*. **nach toirmisgind in lá** "**diem non impedit**" *that does not prevent* (it) *in the day* 13, **ocus toirmisgit in stuider** *and it will prevent the study* 5

Toirthegh *fruit*, **gidhedh is ferr na toirrthi uile do trégin** *nevertheless it is better to shun all fruit* 18, **re gach uili truailleadh tic ona toirthibh** *because of all the pollution which comes of fruits* 18

Tolladh from **tollaim** *I bore, pierce, excavate*, G **toll** *a hole*, W **twll**, Bret **toull**; **arson co tabhair ar an mbiadh tolladh sul dileaghta e** *because it makes the food penetrate* (pass out of the stomach) *before it is digested* 6.

Tosach *the beginning*, G **toiseach**; **uair imcubidh caithme in potaitsi a tosach na coda** *the proper time to use the pottage* (is) *at the beginning of the meal* 23

Tosgaithes from **tosguighim** *I move*, **ocus da tosgadh e began uaithi** *and if it should move* (or depart) *a little from it* (natural custom) 17 **gidhegh mad mór in tosgadh** *nevertheless if the departure* (from nature) *is great* 17, **intan tosgaighius go h'imurcrach** *when it moves superfluously* 5.

Trachtadh, Lat **tractus**, *a tract, treatise*, **sa treas trachtadh** *in the third tract* 11.

Tráth *a time, season*, **tráth ata sa bél** *while* (the time) *it is in the mouth* 8, **trátha muiri** *the times of Mary* 9, **dentur o mhaidin gu tráth** *let it be done in the morning, early* 13

Trátha *Times*, **tratha muiri** *the Hours of Mary* 9

Tréiginus from **tréig** *shun, avoid* **is ro-urus alis na sendaoinibh in tréiginus d'fulang "senes facilime ferunt ieunum"** *the old men most easily bear abstinence* 25

Treorughadh "reductiuum" Inf of **treóruighim** *I guide*—a supremely wise and comprehensive word, **dlighear a treórguhadh tar a ais** *he should or must be guided back*—to his first condition 17, **ocus is e sin a treorughadh cum a contradha** *and that is to lead it towards the contrary* 3

Truaillitt from **truaill** *pollute* **ocus truaillidh in cuimhne** *and it will pollute the memory* 21

Truimidecht *heaviness*, from **trom** *heavy*, W **trwm**, Corn **trom**, Bret **troum**, **gan cuirreneacht na gaothmairecht na truimedecht** *without cramps or flatulence or heaviness* 5, **ocus tromaighi an chorp** *and it will make the body heavy* 7

Tuathadh *the people*, G **tuath**, W **tud**, Bret **tud**, Corn **tus**, Gaul **teut**, akin Lat **totus**, Lett **tauta**; **do reir na tuathadh** *according to the people* 21

Thubhairt Past of **abair** *say* **mar a duburt artús** *as I said at first* 3, **ocus adubhrumar** *and we have said* 3

Tuca *towards them* This is the Scottish Gaelic form for **chuca** as we have **thugad** *towards thee* for the older and etymologically more correct **chugad** and **Cugat**, which see

Tucaoi from **tug**, G **thug** *give*, should be **tuctaoi** 16.

Tuigsin *understanding*, Inf of **tuigim**; **a deirit drong.. a tuigsin an texa sin** *some say. . understanding* (or interpreting) *that text* 2, **ocus is uime sin nach dligher a tuigsin** *and it is therefore it should not be understood* that, etc., 3, **ocus tuicter so o Auicina** *and this may be understood from Avicenna* 13.

Tuilleadh *more*, the Inf. of **tuilim** *I enhance, increase*, **tuilleadh fós** *more yet, furthermore* 14, **misur ina tuillfedh oirett éndige amáin** *the measure* (as much) *as is taken at one drink only* 7.

Tuirlingha *a descent, fall*—based upon an old verb **lingim** *I spring, jump*, **moille tuirlingha** *the slowness* (or delay) *of the falling*—of the food 11.

Tuitim, Inf of **tuitim** *I fall*, **dambia coimplex lenna find ar tuitim do thuithim aicidigh chum fuarachta ocus cum flichada** *and if a general health of pale humors* (perhaps we should say *an anaemic person*) *was fallen to a diseased fall* (or state) *towards coldness and towards moisture* 3, **no go tuitinn an biadh** *until the food has fallen*—into the stomach 6

Tuma from **tum** *dip*, **ocus ar tuma an méir tanuisti and** *and after dipping his second finger in it* 9

Tusga *easier, rather*, **mar is tusga tochluighes an nádur e** *as nature rather desires it* 14.

U

Uachtar *surface, upper part*, **uachtar baindi** *the surface of milk* that is *cream* 23 In Scottish place-names as **Aughter** and **Ochter** the upper ground, **na an uachtar** *or above* 10

Uaigh *a grave*, **ocus rofhurail an uaigh . . . d'oslugadh** *and he commanded the grave to be opened* 28

Uair *an hour, a time*, from Latin **hora**; **uair and** "*time in*"—and out 1, that is, *occasionally*—a pure and peculiarly Gaelic phrase, **toghtar in uair bhus teó** *let the warmer time be chosen* 17, **uair in proinnighthi** *the time of eating*

16, **uair sa mhí** *once a month* 5, **a cét oir** *the first time* 9, **sia huaire** *six times* 15

Ubhal *an apple*, W **afal**, Corn **auallen**, Bret **avallen**—all which suggests a kinship with **Auellana** *the hazel nut*, named upon Avela a town of Campania famous for its fruit, **le croicinn an ubhaill buidhe** *with the skin of the yellow apple* 9—the mange? **mar ata péredha ocus coctana ocus úbhla** *as are pears and coctanas and apples* 18

Uighi *eggs* **dlighear a fis go comhfurtachaoidh na h'uighi ocus a caibhdel in drong bis déis cuisli** *it should be known that the eggs and their custard comfort those who are after blood-letting* 22

Uilidhi, go h'uilidhi *entirely, altogether*, **an aighi . brotha in cuirp go h'uilidhi** *and against eruption of the body generally* 27, **aimsir na bliadhna uile** *the time of the whole year* 21

Uircill *water-melon, pumpkin*, **duille uircill** *the leaf of the melon* 9.

Uireasbhuidh *defect, want of, failure*, **egail uireasbhidh na brighi** *the fear of the failure of the strength* 7

Uirri *upon it*—See **Orra**. This is the Fem sing form

Uisge *water* from a root **ud**, Gk ὑδ-ωρ Sansk **ud-an**, Lat **und-a**; **a h'uisgi fhuar in t'shamradh ocus a h'uisgi the sa geimredh** *out of cold water in the summer and of warm water in the winter* 9

Uisgemail *wateryness* from **Uisge**; **uisegemailmí-tarbhach** *unsubstantial wateryness* 18—See **Tarbhach**

Ullma Compar of **ullamh** *prompt, ready* **air + lamh** *a hand* · *handy* **adeir aueroys gurub ullma . . . leaghtur iarann mór** *A says that (a) large (piece of) iron is sooner or more promptly melted* 2.

Ullmaighim *I prepare, make ready* **ocus ullmuighter a biadh** *and let his food be prepared* 9, **oir ullmuighit nech cum lúbra** *for it prepares* (predisposes) *a person towards leprosy* 12—Note

Umorro *yet, besides, over and above*—the use of the word is not at all definite, but it is always on these lines It occurs frequently, **umorro a deir in fersaighteoir** *and so the versifier says* 21, **an saimradh umorro aimsir ro-te é** *the summer moreover a very hot time it is* 22.

Unsa *an ounce*, here the Troy or pharmaceutical ounce of 480

grains.—See the "signatures" 28, that is, fol. 14*b* of the text.

Urail from **furailim** *I offer, incite.*—See **Furail** in another "side" sense, **ocus ro-(fh)urail eolus ocus áithi bais ocus betha** *and he offered* or taught *the knowledge and prognostics of death and life* 28.

Urbanuis (**Féil**) *the feast of St Urban*; **in samhradh a féil Urbanuis** *in summer in the feast of Urban* 22—May 25th

Urchoid *hurt, harm.* The verb is **urchoidim** *I hurt*, **is ro-mór urchoidighius móran in biadh san oidche** *too much food at night greatly hurts* 14, **urcoidigid na neithi omha** *the raw things hurt* 24.

Urlugadh *vomiting, spewing*, **ocus gan urlugadh na "apititus caininus"** *without vomiting or dog-ish appetite* 5.

Urusa, **gu ro-urusa** *very much easier* The base is **usa** *easier* from Old Irish **asse "facilis"** and **assu "facilius,"** in G as **fasa** Compar of **furasda** *easy.* **Ro-urusa** has a double intensive in it **ro + air + usa** .·. *very much easier*, **truaillter go ro-urusa iad** *they are be-fouled much more readily* 22. There is a further Compar. **innus gumadh usaide tarrong-tar an ní... cum nan ae** *so that the thing* (digested) *is drawn towards the livers* 13, **is usa na boill ele do dileaghadh** *it is easier to digest the other parts* 18,—the other parts are easier to digest, **ni héidir ocus ni h'urusa** *it is not necessary and not easy* 10.

Y

Ypocondria seems altogether out of place here 4 It does not read well into the text and may be disregarded

GLASGOW: PRINTED AT THE UNIVERSITY PRESS BY ROBERT MACLEHOSE AND CO. LTD.